WHEN SPIRITS TOUCH
THE RED PATH

The Red Path Messenger Series

Other Works by the Author

❀

When Spirits Touch the Red Path
Book 1 in the Red Path Messenger Series

The Message
Book 2 in the Red Path Messenger Series

The Season of the Long Shadow
Book 3 in the Red Path Messenger Series

Watchers From the Shadows and The Light
Book 1 in the Watchers Trilogy

The Brotherhood
Book 2 in the Watchers Trilogy

Lumen
Book 3 in the Watchers Trilogy

In Search of Acasia

Desperate Dreams

Keepers of the Beast

WHEN SPIRITS TOUCH THE RED PATH

❁

A Red Path Novel

"Speaking Wind" Patrick Quirk

Dolphin Media, L.L.C.
Huntsville, Alabama

When Spirits Touch the Red Path
A Red Path Novel

Dolphin Media, LLC

For information address:
Dolphin Media, LLC
6275 University Drive, Suite 37
Huntsville, AL 35806

www.dolphinmedia.com

ISBN: 0-9786664-0-2

Printed in the United States of America

This book is dedicated to my son Timothy. May you live and mature well so you will be capable of understanding your life. Remember, not all things are as they appear at first. There is a more complete meaning to the life path you have set before you than you may understand now. Think of these things I am presenting to you even after you have set the book down and listen for the truths that come to you from those very knowledgeable voices within you as they have come to me. Those same voices have always been with us but are so often ignored.

With love,

Dad

Contents

❀

Part V   When the Spirit Sees

Part VI   A Spirit's Touch

Part VII   Journey Through the Spirit Painting

Part VIII The Spirit Lights

Part IX   A Place of Remembering

Part X   A Whisper Through Time

Part XI   A Gathering of Visions

Part XII   A Place Called Beginning

Foreword

❀

We come into this life path of the Earth Mother with two separations. We have first been separated from the Great Spirit and we have been separated from the other half of us. It is our spiritual quest to rejoin the Great Spirit with all that we have set before us to accomplish. It is the quest of a life path to be prepared to meet our other half spirit so we will understand what we have accomplished and gain insight into what we must still do…together…and as one.

Two Bears, Spirit Caller
From The Land of the Pueblos
1947 A.D.

Acknowledgements

❀

Cover layout and design by Cliff Collier and Jim King.
Photo on front cover by Marilyn "Angel" Wynn.
Photo on back cover by Bryan Rohbock.
Edited by the author, Sharon Dooling and Jim King.

Introduction

❀

Grandfather had brought Cheeway and me to the top of the mesa that was just outside of Albuquerque, New Mexico. Not many people came here because Indian legends considered this area to be one of strong medicine. For most of the inhabitants here, that was reason enough to stay away. It was in the late fall of 1960 and we were watching the sun set behind the horizon. The October air was crisp then and what little grass that had been growing in the land was now deep inside its own roots beginning its long sleep for the winter. Grandfather had brought Cheeway and me here to teach us how to listen to the songs of the Earth Mother, as they would be carried by the spirit winds across our lands.

Grandfather had told us that the reason he had brought us here was to be able to explain some things to us that he felt we should know. Cheeway and I were thirteen years old then and did not understand much of what Grandfather would usually tell us, but he would always say that his speaking words would be remembered by both of us and when the time would come for us to have a need for them, they would come to us with a clear understanding that would benefit us as we would gain more seasons to our life paths.

Perhaps our real reason for always accompanying Grandfather at that time was the fact that we just enjoyed listening to all of the stories of our people's past he would tell us then follow up with his own explanation of why they were. In any case, Cheeway and I sat on the ground that was before him. We had prepared ourselves to listen to more of his reasons for having the kind of life path that we all have and how it will all make very good sense once we have crossed from the path of being and onto the one of knowing and understanding.

PART I

❀

THE SPIRIT SONG OF FINDING

CHAPTER 1

❀

Path of the Two Groups

Grandfather positioned himself on one of the large rocks and began his speaking.

"There are those who will care for you and there are those who only remember you. One of them will help you while the other group will hold you back in your advancement of the spirit. However, both of these groups will do what they will because they perceive what they are doing is out of love for you. Do you understand what it is that I am trying to tell you?"

Grandfather had finished his speaking words to us and was looking straight into each of our eyes. We both knew what he would see. He would see that while we were understanding his speaking words for the thoughts that they represented, we did not fully understand what the message was that he was trying to get across to us.

"Both of you must always remember the difference between these two groups and what they will represent to you. On one hand, you will have the ones who care for you. This group will not always be the ones who will give you the warmest of feelings. When they will see that there is a weakness in their perception of what you are doing, they will confront you with this. It will not make you feel very good in the beginning, but later, and as time will pass, you will be able to look back on these encounters and see that what they had told you makes great sense. From these kinds of encounters with this group that cares for you, you will be able to advance your spirit and grow in the direction that is necessary in the life path you are walking with the Earth Mother.

"Now the other group that I have spoken of are the ones who only remember you. This group will always see you either as you were many seasons ago, or they will only accept the good parts about you and will ignore all of the rest. This group will always offer you feelings of kindness and comfort no matter what it is that you are going through. However, I want both of you to remember that this group, even though they also love you, will be responsible for holding you back in the life path you are walking.

"Because this group will only see the good parts of you and will ignore all of the rest, it is only natural to assume that all of the benefit that you will receive from them will be of a temporary nature. While you will receive a good and comforting feeling from them today, when you wake up in the next day, those same problems will still be with you and you will have discovered that nothing has been resolved.

"It becomes very easy to turn away from the constructive criticism of the ones who will care for you. To look at ourselves for who we really are takes great strength and it is the kind of strength that not many who walk a life path possess. When this group, the ones who care for you, tries to help you, your initial reaction is to turn away from them so their speaking words will not reach you. If you turn yourself away from them, you are actually turning away from yourself. Learn to accept all that they will offer you from the love they have for you. You will only grow in your spirit.

"The ones who turn away from this kind of help and assistance, and turn to the group of those who only remember them, will not be able to advance their spirit as well. They will become too dependent on the group who only remembers them for the comfort they are seeking. In time, they will have lost all of the desire and drive that they may have once had in the quest of discovering their true nature and the path that leads to the release of the spirit within them.

"Both of these groups have their place in the balance of understanding the life path that we are all walking. Neither of them should be ignored or held in less respect than the other.

"In both cases, these groups offer you the possibility of increasing the level of understanding that is required by each of us in order to advance our spiritual growth. From the group who cares for you, you will be offered the chance to learn inner strength and courage; and from the group who only remembers you, you will be offered the chance to stop the learning process that allows one's spirit to advance."

I looked over in the direction where Cheeway was sitting. I could tell that he was beginning to understand some of the speaking words that Grandfather had been sharing with us. I, too, was beginning to understand some of what he was saying.

"Grandfather," I asked, looking back in his direction. "What will cause spiritual growth from the group who cares for us?"

"This group will cause spiritual growth in those they love, because they see you as you are. They will tell you all that is true in their eyes for those things you should be doing and what you should not be doing. They will have an inner sense that will show them a spirit picture of you, and if what they see in the present is not similar, they will tell you.

"Now, that in itself is not any reason for causing your spirit to advance. What they will tell you will resound of the sense of truth in all of the speaking words that they will be willing to share with you. Because you will trust them and will feel easy with them, all of the speaking words that they will be willing to share with you will be accepted by you. You will understand, in time, that all which they will share with you, is from the heart and will be offered to you for your own benefit. But this takes work on your part to stay with it.

"When there are words of praise for the things that you have done, this will cause you to stand erect and proud. You will know that what is shared with you in the way of their speaking words is only the truth and you will learn to depend on this. However, when the other side of the love is shared with you, and it is the things that you are either doing wrong or incorrectly, you will feel very sad and even become defensive to their words. If you will learn to call upon the inner strength that is in each of you and face these offerings, not only will your level of understanding grow, but in this process so will your spirit. This will happen because each of you will be able to understand what is happening to you.

"This process is teaching you that there is a balance to your life path. You will not only have accepted the good, or the things that will make you feel good, but it will teach you that you still have much to work on. By facing these truths, you will learn the truth of the path you are walking. This is how you will increase your level of development and understanding and this is how you will advance your spirit to the next higher place. Once you have been able to cross over this threshold of understanding, you will be well on your way to being able to accept yourself as a spirit who will be able to accomplish many great things in the time that has been allotted to you in the life path you both are walking."

CHAPTER 2

❀

Path of the Warrior

"Success in a life path does not come to those who are weak of spirit. It only comes to those who will take on the attributes of the warrior, and the warrior does not rush into or away from any battle without thinking about it first."

"Will we be warriors in this life path that we are walking with the Earth Mother, Grandfather?" Cheeway asked as he continued to sit in the same position that he had originally taken up.

"All who are walking a life path with the Earth Mother must learn the way of the warrior, Cheeway." Grandfather answered, holding his right hand up to both of us.

"The need for the warrior that lives within each of us is not to fight any battles that are on the outside of us. It must learn to fight the battle that continues between the body and the spirit from within each of us. Here is where the attributes of the warrior will come into your life path and it is here that they must be contained.

"We are all continually confronted with two parts of us. One is the body, which is much like a spoiled child and always wanting those things that bring it comfort from the physical world, and there is the spiritual side of us that only requires that we allow it to share the time that has been given to each of us as we walk this life path we are on.

"The battles that continually take place within each of us result from this division and separation of body and spirit. In the beginning of each of our life paths, there are not many battles. The body perceives the spirit as something that is different from itself but it has not yet learned its time is finite. So, it will allow for casual passage of the spirit into its domain. However, as we each pass through more and more seasons, the body becomes aware that it is not only frail but that the amount of time that has been given to it is limited. Once this has happened, it will perceive that the spirit does not have any of these weaknesses and will begin to resent its presence.

"From this point on is where the many battles that take place within each of us will begin. The body will try to convince itself that all that is important will be those things that give it immediate satisfaction. It will attempt to attain these things in any way that it can. This helps to gratify itself but when you will look at this very carefully, you will be able to see that what is transpiring is that the body is trying to hide from its own vulnerability through the gratification that it is able to find.

"Each time the spirit tries to come forward and help in the way of explaining or showing the body things that are necessary for it to understand, the body will try anything within its means to fight the spirit back and to keep its presence unknown.

"Since one of the purposes of walking a life path with the Earth Mother is to learn how to overcome this, the spirit continues its efforts of making its presence known to the body. This results in the many battles that will take place within all of us. It is my greatest hope that when these battles take place within each of you that you will walk away with a higher level of understanding that you had before. It will be in this way, which is the correct path to understanding, that you will be able to see the benefit of overcoming each of the obstacles that will be put before you as you continue to attain the spiritual development that is so necessary to join the Great Spirit and become one once again.

"This is where the warrior is needed in your life path. It is not as many of our people have tried to do in the past by becoming the warrior to those things that were external to them. It is the relationship between the body and the spirit that first created the concept of what the warrior was and it is in this context that I tell the both of you about it.

"The true warriors are aware that most of their life paths occur within themselves. The warrior realizes that the importance of this determines where the majority of effort should lie. Because only the smaller parts of the life path are concerned with those things that are external to themselves, this is the path that does not need as much work even though it is where most of the lessons that create our needed understanding of ourselves comes from."

"Grandfather," I said, looking at him with the most sincere look I could place on my face. "How can this be?"

I could see that Grandfather had stopped what he had been talking about and was looking directly at me. From this look that he had placed on his face, I could tell that he wanted me to continue with my question.

"Grandfather, how can this be when all that we see is on the outside of ourselves. It would seem that these are the places where all of the events of our life path lead us. I do not travel within myself when I must learn something. Just like today, Cheeway and I are listening to the speaking words that you are sharing with us, we are not receiving them from our inside."

"Yes, you are," Grandfather returned. "You are hearing my speaking words with the ears that you have brought with you. However, once my speaking words are heard by you, where do you think that they go to before you can understand them?"

"Then this is what you are referring to as the path that is on our inside, Grandfather?" I asked.

"Yes, Little One, this is the path that holds most of those things that will cause you to advance spiritually.

"Think of this in the way that you would think of your house and all of the things that you perform within it. When your family is in need of food, what do they do? The first thing that they will have to do will be to go out on these lands that have been given to us by the Earth Mother and look for one of her children that is willing to let you eat them. When you have accomplished this, then you will take this meat home with you where it will be prepared into a meal that will allow all of your family to eat it. Is this not correct?"

Both Cheeway and I were able to follow Grandfather's words and were shaking our heads in an up and down manner so that Grandfather would be able to see that we were in agreement with what he was sharing with us.

"So then," Grandfather continued, "it is the same with all that is seen in the outside portion of your life path. The spirit is very knowledgeable but the body is only a traveling vessel. All of the things that you see and do will have to be taken inside of each of you in order for you to learn and understand them. Otherwise, you will become the hunter who will only kill the game and not take it home...and this does not help him or his family at all.

"While the body is very strong, you will think that all of the world that involves you rests on the outside of yourself. It is the unattained and unenlightened person that thinks that all of the meaning to the life path that they are walking is only in what they will see with their eyes. They do not understand that the majority of the life path lessons that will lead to understanding are only to be found within ourselves.

"Now, when you experience a hunger for knowledge and understanding, you will see those things that you will seek in order to achieve this. What happens then is that all of the experience and knowledge that you have found must be taken inside of yourself in order for it to be prepared so that it will make sense to you. If this is not done, then there is nothing gained from any of it. It will pass you by in the same way that a conversation that you do not understand does.

"Remember this, both of you. People who do not frequently travel the path that leads to spiritual advancement do not recognize that only a small part of all that is necessary to achieve success in their life path resides on the outside of them. They will not be aware of all things that come to them. However, a person who is traveling a life path in the correct way will realize that most all that is needed resides within. They will become completely aware of all things that come to them. These are the people you should seek out to learn from in the life path you are both walking. From them, you will be able to learn and understand great things that are available to all that are within the domain of the Earth Mother.

"This will serve both of you very well in the seasons that will pass before you. This will be how you will know a person for what their intentions will be and will know far in advance what truths their speaking words will hold for you."

"Grandfather," I asked still sitting in the same position that I had started in, "does this apply to all who will cross our life paths?"

"Yes, it does," he replied. "There is no difference in those who are walking a life path today from those who have walked a life path with the Earth Mother many generations before. You will see great improvements in the way that people live and how they will accomplish the things that must be done in order to have food to eat and shelter from the spirits of the land. But the way to understanding the balance of the life path does not change nor do the lessons that must be learned."

"Then it would be better if we stayed away from these people when we saw them?" Cheeway asked Grandfather, adjusting his sitting position a little.

"It would be nice if we could, Cheeway. However, you will find that as you increase the number of seasons that you will pass through, it will become inevitable that you will have to encounter many of them along the way. The best thing for you to do in such situations is to understand them. Listen to them with the understanding that they are only slightly awake. This will help you to overlook many of the things that they will try to tell you or convince you of.

"For the most part, they mean no harm, but they will do and say the things that they do because they do not know any better. To them, there is only one way in their life path and that is their way. Because they do not have anything of truth that they can hold onto, they will try very hard to convince you that their way is correct. However, this is only for their benefit. What they are trying to do is to show you their efforts of putting up with all of the confusion that they are experiencing in the life path they are walking.

"Once you understand this, it will be easier for you to let their speaking words fall to the ground beneath you. When you understand this, you will become one of the untouchable spirits who knows their direction and will not be side tracked by others who know only confusion."

"But, Grandfather," I said. "If these people are so confused and misdirected, could we not stop for awhile to help them?"

"To stop and try to help them would be a terrible risk. However, it is not a task that is impossible, but it has the same dangers as helping a drowning man in the water. If you jump in and try to offer assistance to him but he is not willing to stop all of his own efforts of trying to stay on top of the water, it is very possible that he will not only drown himself, but you as well, in the process. If this man can be made to stop all of his efforts and movements, then the chances of you saving his life are much greater and both of you will be able to reach the ground safely.

"This is the same with all of those people who you will both encounter in the life path that has been set before you. The only way that you will be able to help them is if they will be willing to give up on the direction that they are going and sit still for you. If they cannot do this and you have stopped to help them, then the result will always be that they will drag you down to their level of the life path they are walking and you will end up in their position."

"Grandfather," I said. "Cheeway and I have seen many of the other men of our village who have the same number of seasons on them as you do, but they do not look like you do. Some of them walk bent over and do nothing but complain and others of them cannot even walk. You on the other hand are able to climb tall cliffs and mountains with us and do not tire as quickly as we do. Does this have anything to do with the speaking words that you are sharing with us as well?"

"Yes, it does. What you will understand in this life path is what you will become. If you continually fight the spirit that lives within you, the scars of all of those battles will show. This is what has happened to those men of our village that you speak of. If you learn to accept the majority of the lessons that will come to you and be comfortable with it, then you will not have to fight so many battles. The benefits will be in having a stronger and healthier life path to walk with the Earth Mother while you are learning to understand all that has been set before each of you.

"From the moment that you make your decision on which path you will be willing to take, your spirit will be able to do much of the work for you. It will bring you into many situations that you will be able to learn and gain insight from. After this, you will find that your level of understanding will increase with each day that you will have the opportunity of walking through."

CHAPTER 3

❀

Two Spirits on the Mesa

Finishing his speaking words to us, Grandfather sat silently on the rock where he had positioned himself. Cheeway and I followed his action and sat in silence ourselves. We listened to the sound of the spirit wind as it was crossing our lands, carrying the messages of the Earth Mother to all of her children. We were deep within ourselves, thinking of all that Grandfather had shared with us.

Through the sounds of the spirit wind that was crossing our lands, we heard the faint sound of flutes and drums playing a melody that was not familiar to either of us, but we could tell that it was in the form of a spirit song. When we heard it, we looked over to the position where Grandfather was sitting and see by the look that was on his face that he had heard it as well.

Slowly, it began to get louder until it became very obvious to all three of us that it was not a noise that we were imagining.

When the music seemed to reach its full volume, I could tell that it was coming from the top of one of the large rocks that was close to us. I looked up and saw that there were two people standing there. They were not making any sounds that I could hear but I could tell that it was a man and a woman and they were holding each other very tenderly.

They were dressed in the traditional clothing that was worn by our people many generations ago. I knew this because Grandfather had shown us pictures of what our people dressed like in those times. I was wondering why these strange acting figures were dressed as they were.

As they looked at each other, they began to sing to the melody that was playing in the background. It was one of the most beautiful songs I have ever heard.

Each of the two figures stood facing the other one and I could tell that what I was seeing in them was a great love for each other. As they faced the other, the song intensified and within a few moments, I thought that it was loud enough to be heard over all of our people's lands.

The song and the music that had accompanied it stopped as suddenly as it had begun. There was a silence that came over this land but it was not a silence that was empty. I could feel that a comforting fullness had filled all of the lands that were around us. I turned to look at Cheeway and Grandfather to see if they, too, were perceiving this. Satisfied that they had this feeling, I turned back to look at the two who were standing on the top of the rock but when my sight returned to the place where they had been standing, they were no longer there. The only remaining trace of their visit was the warm feeling that was residing inside of me.

In anticipation of hearing Grandfather share his speaking words to us, I looked over in his direction. When he came into my sight, I saw that there were great streams of water rolling down over his face. Both Cheeway and I knew that this experience had been understood by Grandfather but he needed his privacy. We continued to sit in our positions in silence and with our faces turned away from him so he would have the time that he would require.

Later in the evening, Grandfather had still not found it necessary to share any of his speaking words to either of us and silently rose from his position making signs of the hands that it was time for us to leave. We could see that his heart was very heavy this day but we knew that when the time was right, he would share his understanding of this event with us so we would be able to learn from it as well.

Several months later, Cheeway and I were exploring an old Indian village. We were out of school for a week, and had decided to explore the mesa that was very close to the position where we had the encounter with Grandfather. We had been walking over this area about one year ago and had accidentally discovered an old Indian village. It had been worn down by ages of wind and dust storms. Had we not been walking in the area, I do not believe that we would have noticed it was there. Now, what once had been a large and thriving village, remained as a dust laden grouping of foundations from where its houses had once stood.

It had taken us most of the day to get to the place of the old village and we had brought provisions that would last us through the night. Walking up to the edge of the village, we stopped and looked at what it had turned into. We were rebuilding it in our minds in the way we thought it may have looked when it was inhabited.

From the people we had talked to prior to coming here, we were told that the last people to live here walked among the children of the Earth Mother over five hundred years ago. No one knew much about them and at the time, not many people cared enough to try and find out more about the original inhabitants. Consequently, we were looking at a village that had remained untouched for the most part from the time the last inhabitant left.

Looking at what was left of the buildings that had been here, their mud foundations told us the general location of the houses. We were looking at a particular formation in the middle of the ruins. The buildings here seemed to be formed into a circle but there was not a trace of anything that had been built in the center of them. Being the curious types, we decided that we should begin our explorations in this center of the old village. Perhaps we would discover something valuable that we would be able to impress Grandfather with.

As we were walking in the center of the circle, I told Cheeway that I had a funny felling about being here. I felt like someone was trying to tell me something or to look in a certain place but I could not make out the words that clear. He looked at me and said with a laugh that I needed to put on my hat because the sun was beginning to have an effect on me.

We each went to separate positions within this circle to see if there were any clues why there had not been any building in it. As we were looking close at the ground, small pieces of dust were beginning to fly into our eyes and mouths. A small wind had begun to blow but it was nothing more than a nuisance to us in our exploration of these ruins.

Within a few moments through, the wind was beginning to gain in strength and as I looked over to the horizon, I could see that there were big black clouds coming our way from the north. We decided to set up our tents within the shelter of one of the big rocks, then would continue our exploration of the area. We knew that if the dust became too bad, we could always wait it out from the inside of our tents. We also knew that this time of the year, the rain would not come this far south so that did not pose a threat to us.

Having set up our tents and anchored them down, we returned to the center of the built up circle where our interests had been perked earlier. The dust that was being kicked up by the winds now had become very strong and was diffusing the sunlight into a yellow haze caused by the reflection of the light against the brown sand in the air. The force of the wind was getting to be very strong now and we could feel it, as it would try to push us from one place to the other. I looked at Cheeway and saw that he was covered in the fine powder and would seem to make a dust trail out of our movements in the wind as it would take a little off of him then put a whole bunch more back on again.

Through all of this, I was still picking at the idea that something was trying to tell me something. I was standing at the bottom of the outside of the circle we were working in when it suddenly came to me. There was something that was just under my feet. Looking down, I could only catch quick glimpses of the ground when it was not being hidden from my view by the blowing sand. Looking at those few glimpses, I did not notice anything unusual and was wondering if I was thinking about things that were not there for me to see.

Within a few moments of trying to see what it was that was under my feet, it dawned on me that whatever it was might be under the ground and not on the top of it. I looked around for one of the shovels we had with us. Peering through the orange glow the sunlight was making in this dust storm, I could make out one of the shovels over by the tents. I decided that this was the spot I wanted to dig in and placed a marker on it so I could return to this same spot with the shovel. I proceeded in the direction of the tent and braced myself backward against the wind so I would not be blown forward. Uncovering whatever it was that was under the dirt here was gradually becoming an obsession to me and I had decided to continue my search in spite of the dust storm, which had not reached a high fevered pitch.

Reaching the tent, I heard Cheeway yelling for me to come in before I was blown away. I ignored his words and, picking up the shovel, I leaned forward into the wind and fought my way back to the place I had just marked. I felt the small stings from the sand that were blowing in my face and pulled my outer shirt over my head for protection. Looking through one of the button holes in the shirt, I watched for my marker to appear as I pushed myself into the direction of the wind, feeling its strength blowing against me.

I reached the marker I had left in the middle of the circle. I tied my outer shirt over my face and positioned my back so it was against the wind. Then I began to dig in the soil that was beneath my feet. Each shovel of dirt that I would dig out of the ground was bringing me closer to what I was looking for I could feel it.

The dust storm was now strong enough that I did not have to throw the dirt far away. I would only have to toss it out of the shovel and into the air, then the wind would do the job of taking it away from the spot I was digging. Each shovel of dirt I would take out of the hole was replaced by some of the dust that was blowing in but it was not sufficient to impair my progress substantially. I continued digging and was able to block the fact that there was a strong dust storm around me.

The hole I was digging was now large enough for me to stand in and it provided a small shelter against the blowing sand that was being shot at me by the wind. I was feeling better now that the constant barrage of sand particles had subsided as I continued to work in the hole I had dug. I continued to dig and could see that I was making very good progress.

The digging had taken my mind off all other things that were happening around me. Because of this lack of attention, I was very surprised to feel something jump down into the hole with me. As I turned around, I was very relieved to see that it was Cheeway who had come to join me. He told me that the reason he was in the hole with me now was because the wind had just blown both of our tents away and this hole was the only place that offered him any shelter at all. With the wind and dust trying to cover us from above, we both picked up our shovels and began to dig. He asked me what it was I was digging for, and all I could do was turn to him, shrug my shoulders and say "just something I know is here".

We had been digging for about an hour when our shovels hit solid rock. Thinking that it was a large boulder, we tried to dig around it but found that it went further than the boundaries of the hole we had dug. The hole we had dug was about seven feet deep now and the last thing we wanted to do was to begin digging from the top of it in order to widen it. The dust storm would not have treated us well if we had done that. Instead, we began to scrape off the top dirt to make a determination of just how big this rock was.

Once we had scraped off the top soil, we could see that it was not a rock we had uncovered at all. It looked like a hand chiseled door that had been placed over a hole for some reason. Looking at the piece of hand worked stone, we saw what could have been two handles that were on two of its ends. We each took a handle of this door and lifted with all of the strength that we could find within ourselves. With more strength than we ever thought was in us, we were able to lift off the top of this covering—and saw that there was a large black open pit under it.

Fortunately, Cheeway had brought our flashlights. Turning them on, we looked for the bottom of the black pit below us and could see that the floor was approximately five or six feet from the opening. After shining our lights around the hole, we were convinced that there was nothing in there that could do us any harm. We had decided to go into the hole, but only one of us at a time, and only after we had our rope that we had brought with us.

I was the one who went back to where the tents used to be and retrieved the rope. Getting back to the hole, I was also the one that was to go into the pit to see what was there. We had tied one end of the rope to Cheeway's waist, then dropped it down the hole where I would soon follow it in. We performed a few tests first though in order to make sure that my friend would be able to pull me back out of this pit once I was in it. He stood out of the hole we had just dug and we made two practice escapes out of it. Convinced that he could pull me out of the pit, I made my entry.

Entering the pit, I stood motionless for a few minutes as my eyes adjusted to dark surroundings. Once I could see the light from the hole above us, I turned on my flashlight and let its beam roam the pit I was in.

Looking first at the floor, I saw that there were pieces of pottery that had been set around and some stones that had been placed in the middle of the pit that could have been used for a fire place. Shining my light on the walls, I saw that there were crude paintings of animals and people and all of them seemed to be performing some function or another. Casually looking at what had been left in this pit, I was wondering if these had actually been left here by the original inhabitants. If they had, they would have to have been left here over five hundred years ago. As that thought was sweeping its way through my mind, I lost my footing on one of the stones that was in the middle of the room and fell backwards. As I fell, the flashlight slipped from my hand and landed to where it was shining on a piece of the wall that was close to the ceiling.

I was stunned by what I saw in this portion of the wall. Someone had painted the same scene that we had been through on the mesa only a few months ago. Thinking that it was done recently, I rushed over to the position it was located on the wall and touched it. The paint was so dry and it began to crumble off onto my fingers when I felt it. I knew that this was not done in recent times and that it was at least as old as the rest of the things in this pit.

I looked carefully at this painting and noticed that the colors and type of paint used to create this were different than the ones used to create the others on the wall. This picture also had been painted with a border around it and this made it stand out even more from the other painted pictures on the wall. Looking closer at the painting, I noticed that there were no faces on the two individuals but they did have on the same clothing that they had been wearing when they made their presence known to the three of us. These two individuals looked exactly the same as when we had seen them on the mesa only a few months earlier.

Behind them was a painting of a sunset and some of the most brilliant colors went into portraying the clouds that were in it. At the very bottom of the picture and just beyond the lower border, there was the picture of the back of someone's head looking at them as they were standing in front of the sunset. This picture was very familiar to me because this was just the thing I had experienced only a few months ago. If this picture had been painted over five hundred years ago by the original inhabitants of this village, I knew that we could not have been the first one they had visited, and from the speaking words that Grandfather had shared with us in matters such as these, I knew that there must be a reason for Cheeway and I to have been brought to this place. But how could they look the same now as they did then?

I shined the light to the right and left of the picture and saw that there were more paintings with the borders on them but they all seemed to be limited to this small location within the pit. I was about to walk closer to their positions to examine them further when I heard Cheeway call my name. The tone of his voice was rushed and I could tell that he was getting very excited about something. He was pulling on the rope with such a sense of urgency, I thought he would pull it completely out of the pit that I was in.

Walking over to the opening of the pit, I heard the sound of thunder. It was so loud that it was shaking some of the dirt from the hole we had dug into the pit. Cheeway was frantic and by the time I saw him standing at the entrance, his eyes were so wide open that I thought they would fall out. His voice rang with the quivering of excitement as he shouted to me that we had to leave this place right now!

Grabbing the rope, I began climbing out of the pit. Once I had reached him, I asked Cheeway why he was so excited about leaving and what the urgency was. Stepping on the door as it lay on its side, we both looked out the hole we had dug, he simply pointed his finger to the north and told me to look. As I looked out of the hole, I was shocked to see that huge black clouds were over us and it had begun to rain. This was not the normal New Mexico rain on the mesa, but it was like a monsoon. The rain was coming down so hard, I could see waves of water in the air as it was rushing toward the ground. The ground was not able to absorb such an amount of water and it was trying to push it back and send it somewhere else.

Before I had time to study the situation, I heard Cheeway shout to me that if we did not get out of the hole, we would be trapped. Looking at him, I saw that he was attempting to scale the wall of the hole we had dug but as he was attempting to get out of the hole, water was pouring in over him and causing the earth to flood the hole we were standing in. We frantically scrambled to get out this hole we had dug before it would bury us with all of the soil we had just taken out of it.

Our hands were desperately searching for anything to hold on to that would allow our arms and legs to push us up from the inside of this hole. Each time we thought we had a hold of something, the water would come pouring down over us and wash our hand hold away. We felt the futility of our situation in this hole and thought that this was our end. Finally, some common sense reached our minds and we decided that I should push Cheeway up from the hole since he already had the rope tied to his waist. Then, once he was out of the hole, he would be able to pull me up.

I bent down in the hole to grab one of his feet, which would give me the needed leverage to push him out of the hole. As I reached for one of his feet, the mud was so slick that it made my hands slide off and I could not get a solid grip on either of them. After several attempts and dozens of gallons of water and mud later, one of his feet had been washed sufficiently by the water pouring into the hole with us that I could grasp it firmly enough to push him out of the hole. Soon, I could see the top of his head as he was standing at the top of the hole and was holding the rope out to me. I grabbed the rope and began to pull myself up from the hole. Just as I was about half way out of the hole, a bolt of lightening struck about ten feet away from where we were. The shock of the thunder was so strong that it knocked my friend over and rolled me back into the hole we were trying to get out of.

As I rolled back into the hole, I began sliding on the slick mud that the dirt had turned into and I saw that I was heading in the direction of the opening to the pit I had just explored. I knew that if I were to slide into the pit, that Cheeway would not be able to get me out of it again, so I was frantically reaching and grabbing for anything that would stop my direction into the pit. Grabbing into the mud, my hands were not able to find anything that would hold me sufficiently to stop my forward direction in my slide. Each time I would begin to slow down my sliding momentum in the mud, more water would come rushing into the hole and speed me up again. I could see the opening to the pit biting at my feet now.

Just as I was about to be washed into the pit, my mind handed me a thought. I responded to it by stretching myself across the opening using both my legs and arms as cross beams. I stretched my legs and arms out until they were supporting me from all four points of the opening. I was facing up and could see waves of water and mud as they were rushing into the hole with me. However, I did not see Cheeway anywhere at the top of the hole.

I could feel the strength in my arms and legs leaving me and I knew that I could not hold this position much longer. Soon, I would be washed into the blackness of the pit below me with all of the water and mud that was rushing in. The storm outside was not going away, and from the sounds of it I could tell that it was still increasing in its strength.

What seemed like an eternity of minutes later, I was relieved to see Cheeway's face looking over the edge of the hole we had dug and he was yelling to me that I should grab the rope. I could only look for the rope sparingly because when I opened my eyes for any period of time, the mud would rush into them and I would have to close them again. Finally, I saw the rope. It was waving to me just over my left shoulder. My first attempt to reach the rope with my left had almost resulted in my being pulled into the pit because my weight distribution did not allow for any one of the four points of resistance to be moved. Shifting my weight a little, I attempted to reach out for the rope once again. This time, I was successful. I had a hold on the rope and immediately grabbed it with my other hand.

Having both hands on the rope now, I was clinging onto it for all I was worth but I did not have any strength left that I could pull myself up the rope with. I could only hope to hold onto the rope to keep from being pulled into the pit below me until the rain had stopped. I could feel that the coldness from the rain and the mud had made my hands almost numb and I was beginning to lose my grip on the only thing that was keeping me from entering the pit.

Suddenly, with more force than I knew Cheeway was capable of, I was being pulled out of the hole. The force was so strong that I was being buried under the mud and water that was rushing into the hole. I felt like there were at least one or two feet of the stuff over the top of me now but I continued to move out of the hole. As I was being pulled, I was trying to assist the efforts by using my feet to push me up as well. I could feel that this was merely a gesture because they too had lost their strength. I was a lump of flesh now and I could only hope that my friend did not loose his momentum with me at the end of this rope.

At long last, I felt the incline level out and I knew that I was out of the hole. I was trying to roll myself away from the opening because if more water loosened the dirt around the hole, I could be back in the same predicament I had just gotten out of.

I was beginning to roll when I felt hands grab me. It was not the two hands I had been anticipating, but it was several groups of them and they pulled me away from the hole. Looking up to see who had given me this assistance, I was surprised to see three other people. Before I could say anything, I heard a slurping sound from where I had just come from. Wiping the mud out of my eyes, I looked over to the direction of the hole, I saw that the force of the water had been too much for the ground and the hole we had dug was now caving in on itself.

Within minutes of being pulled from this hole, it was no longer in existence. There was not one trace that it had ever been there. If I were still in it, there would have been no trace of me either. Sitting there in the rain, it felt good to have the mud wash off from me. I looked over at Cheeway and saw a very wet and smiling face. He asked me if I was all right. I told him that I was and asked him where these other people had come from. He told me that just as he had gotten out of the hole, he saw a truck driving through the rainstorm and he had left our position to get some help from them.

He had run towards them and was not sure they had seen him. He told me that was when the lightning hit and lit the ground so well that they stopped their truck just long enough for him to reach it and ask for their help. I looked at him and, puzzlingly, asked him if he could have been in two places at once? All of their faces lit with a surprised expression and my friend asked me what I meant.

I told him that I saw him trying to pull me out of the hole when the lightning hit and that was what knocked him over and me back into the hole. He looked at me and said, "That was not I, I was too far away by then."

The driver of the truck put his hand on my shoulder and said that what my friend was telling me was true. Who was it then, I asked? But none of them had seen anyone else around the hole I was in.

The other two in the truck had come back with a tarp shelter and set it up between two of the larger rocks. After building a small fire and warming ourselves, we introduced ourselves to each other. I learned that the driver of the truck's name was Joe Sitting Dog and he and his two sons had been driving from the town back to the reservation where they lived. Normally, they would not have driven past this place because their tribe considered it to have big medicine and the others did not want to come by it. Because of the dust storm that day, Joe had decided that he would risk it because it meant that he would be home twenty minutes earlier.

"It was fortunate for you that we came this way," Joe said.

Joe said that there were many legends about this land here and that they were too real for him to ignore. He said that when he was a young man, he was out hunting with his Grandfather. One of the rabbits they were after had gone into this area. When they went after it, they came across this same village but just before they were about to enter the center of the village, the place we had dug our hole, they were stopped by a man and a woman.

"The man and woman just stood there looking at the both of us," Joe Sitting Dog continued, "and I saw my Grandfather's face turn into fear. We left then, and until this day, I had not ever come back and my Grandfather did not ever talk about it, other than telling me not to ever come back to this place because the medicine here was too strong."

Joe Sitting Dog did admit to being curious about the people who once lived here. He said that according to the tribe's legends that had been handed down, the last people who lived here vanished somewhere between five to eight hundred years before and did not leave anything behind them when they left. He told us that every now and then this part of our lands would be covered with a cloud that would be so thick that you could not see through it. His people believed that this was where the Earth Mother gave birth to her clouds that would bring the rain we needed so much.

"Because of this and the sightings," Joe continued, "we always left this land alone, because we considered it sacred to the Earth Mother who has always taken care of us."

Sitting next to the small fire, I could feel my body beginning to come back to life. As I welcomed the warmth from the fire, I sat there looking out from under the tarp that was sheltering us from the rain and into the land that was being drowned in the fierce rainstorm…and I thought. I was thinking about the visit I had in this same area just a few months ago, finding the same picture on the wall of the pit that had been painted several hundred years ago, who it could have been that was holding me up on the rope when Cheeway went to get help, and how fortunate I was to be here now and breathing.

PART II

❀

THE SPIRITS JOURNEY

CHAPTER 4

❀

Face of the Spirit

It had been several days since Cheeway and I had our experience on the land of the mesa. We both had time to get over our exhaustion and the fear of what a close call we both had. I had been sitting on the front porch of my parents' house, thinking of those events of the last few days when out of the corner of my eyes, I saw that Cheeway had walked over to the front of our fenced in yard and was calling to me with his thoughts.

This was a very considerate way of asking the person and spirits who lived in the house for their acceptance before entering. Grandfather had always made sure that both of us would learn the polite ways of our people and this was one of them. There was another advantage to this kind of exercise though, and that was that it helped us to exercise our minds as well. Grandfather had always told us that when we could recognize those who were close to us in this life path with the Earth Mother, then we would be able to recognize them when they needed our assistance but were not able to be seen by us.

It would be in this way, he would always tell us, that the majority of assistance would be rendered to those who were in trouble. Trouble, he would often tell us, did not wait for the convenience of having those who would need you be close. He said that the mind was only a physical extension of the spirit. When we would be able to recognize this picture of the mind within ourselves, that would be the first step toward it.

I could see Cheeway standing at the outside of the fenced in area of our land and looking at him, I decided to close my eyes and search for the face of his spirit that was calling to me. I closed my eyes and found that initially, there was nothing for me to see. However, as I sat there in silence and attempted to clear my own mind of all that was in it, I began to notice that there was a feeling of a small presence. Once I noticed that, it began to grow.

Soon, I was able to recognize that it was Cheeway. However, it was not a face that was coming to me, it was a feeling. As this feeling grew within me, and I accepted it as Cheeway's, I attempted to create a place within my mind that would take a picture of this so I would be able to call on it when it would be necessary.

I knew that with this picture of what Cheeway looked like to me in the spirit, I would be able to recognize him when he would next call on me. I wanted to test this and after holding up my right hand to him which was the signal he was waiting for to come onto our land, I decided to tell him about this great discovery that I had just made from him.

We sat down under the small pine tree that was planted in the front of our house and I unfolded the experiences that I had just received from him.

"Is Grandfather home, Cheeway?" I asked, as I was seating myself under the small pine tree.

"I do not know. When I passed his house, I did not see his truck parked in the front."

"We really need to talk to him, Cheeway. Not only about the event that had happened to us on the mesa, but also to tell him about the strange painting that I saw in the hole from the old village."

"Grandfather has been acting very strange for the last couple of days," Cheeway continued with his speaking words, as he too was trying to adjust himself among the rocks and dirt that was beneath us. "I, too, want to ask him these questions and to better understand what he can share with us. However, I simply have not seen him since the day we were all together on the land of the mesa."

"Cheeway," I said, as I leaned forward and touched his right shoulder with my left hand, "Do you know what I was doing when you were standing in the front of the fence thinking of me and wishing to be invited onto our land?"

I could see that Cheeway did not have any idea of what it was that I was going to tell him but since I saw that I had his attention, I decided to continue with my explanation.

"I was trying to see what you looked like in my mind."

"But you know what I look like. We have known what each other has looked like for all of our lives."

"You do not quite understand what it is that I am trying to say, Cheeway. I was not trying to remember what you look like on the outside. I was trying to see what you looked like in my mind when you were thinking of me and wanting me to invite you onto our land."

"OK, so what do I look like?" Cheeway asked, in a rather annoyed tone of voice.

"I did not see you, Cheeway."

"So you were not successful in what you were trying to do?"

"Yes, I was very successful, Cheeway. I said that I did not see you, but I did see your spirit."

When I said this, I could see Cheeway's face turn a bright color of red. He was leaning so far forward that I felt that he was going to fall over with only the slightest of pushes.

"You know," Cheeway said to me in a very low whisper, "this had been done only by the wise ones."

"I know, Cheeway. However, I believe that once I explain how I accomplished this in my mind, then you, too, will be able to perform such a feat."

"To what end will this serve us? I mean, with so many things that we need to ask Grandfather about, why should we try to learn something that we can always come back to at a later time?"

"Cheeway," I said leaning forward myself, "this will be how we will find Grandfather. Or better yet, this will be how we will call Grandfather to us since we cannot find him."

I could see by the look that was coming over Cheeway's face that he was catching onto the gist of things now, and he was in complete agreement with me.

"What must we do first?" Cheeway asked.

"The first thing that we must do is as I did to get the spirit picture of you. Close your eyes now and let me try to talk us both through this sequence of events that brought you to my mind. Once we have done this, then we can learn how Grandfather looks to us as a spirit."

Both Cheeway and I closed our eyes and cleared our minds of all things that we could find in them. Once this was accomplished, we then concentrated on the sound of the small breeze that was carrying the Earth Mother's messages through the little pine that was planted in the front of our yard. As we listened to it relaying the messages of the children of the Earth Mother to the spirit wind, we found ourselves hearing its messages becoming louder to both of us.

With a very short time, this was the only sound that we could hear. Now, it was time for Cheeway and I to try to feel each other in our minds. I had told him that once we had cleared our minds and could only hear the sounds of the spirit wind carrying its messages, that this would be the time when both of us would begin to concentrate on the other one until we could feel the spirit image of the other come into our minds. Once this occurred, then we would open our eyes and look at the other one to let them know when we had accomplished our task.

We had been in a clear mind under the small pine tree for about twenty minutes when I could feel the spirit of Cheeway come to me. Once this was accomplished, I opened my eyes and saw that his were already opened and he was looking at me with a very surprised look on his face.

"What did we just do?" Cheeway asked me, with a look of confusion coming over his face.

"We did the same thing that I told you I did with you when you were standing outside the of the fence, Cheeway. We have just picked up the other's spirit thought and image."

"Do you mean that this is how we look as spirits?" Cheeway asked.

"I do not know if this is how our true spirit bodies will look when the time comes for us to cross over the great spirit waters to the waiting place, Cheeway. I can only say that this must be how they look to us as we are walking a life path with the Earth Mother now. Tell me, Cheeway, what did you see?"

"It was not that I really saw anything at all," Cheeway explained. "It was rather what I felt. I could feel something that was coming into my mind that I knew as you. It is very difficult to explain but as near as my speaking words can relate to it, it was like feeling the presence of you in my mind. I am sure that if I had wanted to, I could have given you a form that would have been easier to relate to. But it happened so quickly, I only accepted the feeling of you in the way that I accept your speaking words to me when I remember things that we have shared when we are not together."

"Let's try it again, Cheeway," I offered. "But this time let us both try to give the other one a message. It must be a message that neither one of us can know. Once we have made this contact once again, we will tell the other one what it was that we were thinking of and see how close it was."

Cheeway was in agreement with this and once again, we emptied our minds of all things that we could think of and listened to the spirit wind carrying the messages of the Earth Mother until we could hear nothing else.

When we had completed this process once again and had made our initial contact, I opened my eyes to look at Cheeway at the same time that he had opened his to look at me. I could see that the look on his face was the same as it was on mine. What had occurred had surprised both of us and we were not taking any measures of hiding it from the other one.

"What did you think I was telling you, Cheeway?" I asked, feeling a little surprised by the turn of events that had just happened.

"I did not get that far," Cheeway said, as he continued to look at me with a wild kind of look on his face.

"What do you mean, Cheeway?"

"As soon as I had cleared my mind and heard only the sound that the wind spirit was making as it was carrying its messages from the Earth Mother, I thought that I was picking up the message that you were sending to me. However, as I waited for it to make itself known to me, I saw a face of an old man. His face was larger that what I could see. I became very scared of this and I do not know why. But in any case, when I opened my eyes to come back, I saw that you were opening yours at the same time. What did you see?"

I could see that Cheeway was not going to let go of this line of questioning until I had given him the answers he was looking for and because he had been so open with me, I felt no shame in telling him that I, too, was frightened.

"I could feel that his eyes were looking right through me," I said, "and I wanted to come back as fast as I could. However, just as I began to open my eyes and leave this place I was in, I heard him give speaking words to me."

"I did not have any speaking words come to me. What did you hear from him?" Cheeway asked me, sitting straight up now.

"Just as I was about to open my eyes and come back to this place, the face looked at me and with a new look of kindness, he said 'Call Grandfather Now!'"

"What do you think that we should do then?" Cheeway asked, sitting in a position of knowing what would be coming next but not wanting to do it.

"I believe that we must perform this process once again, Cheeway; and once we are in the correct position of our minds, we must call to Grandfather, just like the face told me that we should do."

"What if the face should come back to us again?"

"I do not believe that it will, Cheeway. After all, we are doing what he had told us to do, aren't we?"

Cheeway did not completely believe in what we were going to do and I could see this by the look that he was presenting to me on his face. However, I could tell that he would do what was required of him because Grandfather had instructed us both that when the spirits of the land would come to us and instruct us to perform a task, then we must perform it. The reason that they had for it would be for the best of reasons even if we could not see them then.

"How shall we do this?" Cheeway asked.

"I really do not have any ideas of what is correct or what is not correct, Cheeway, but I believe that whatever we will do from this point on will be with the assistance of the spirits of the land because we are attempting to perform what they have asked of us.

"There is one thing that I believe that we should do as soon as we are able to clear our minds and only hear the spirit wind carrying its messages through our lands. That is when we are at this point in our minds, we should put Grandfather's face deep within our own minds. Once this picture is formed by the both of us, we should send it up and into the spirit wind who will carry it to wherever Grandfather is."

"How do you know this?" Cheeway asked.

"I do not know, Cheeway. These are thoughts that were being given to me as I was sharing them with you. It felt like I was not the one who was sharing these speaking words with you. It was almost like I, too, was hearing them for the first time."

"They do seem to be very good speaking words though," Cheeway said. "I believe that you were given them because it is what we are supposed to do."

"I also believe this, Cheeway."

Once again, both Cheeway and I repeated the steps to set our minds into the state that had brought us many experiences that day. As we did this, we both brought with us our image of Grandfather to this new place in our minds that we found. Once we both had the picture of Grandfather in our minds, we released it to the spirit wind. As we let out our air, we could both feel the image of Grandfather going off with all of the other messages that the spirit wind was carrying with it.

We repeated this process several times during that day and as we continued to perform this ceremony, we completely lost track of time until we were interrupted by someone's hand touching each of us on the shoulder.

When we felt a hand on our shoulders, we were brought immediately back to our senses. Opening our eyes, we looked up and saw that it was Grandfather who was standing over both of us and giving each of us a very stern look.

"And just what have the two of you been up to that has brought me here so abruptly?" Grandfather asked, pulling his hands from our shoulders and placing them on both of his hips.

"Well, Grandfather," I said, in the most respectful tone of voice I could come up with. "We needed to speak to you but no one could find you."

"Did it ever cross either of your minds that I, too, might have been very busy doing something as well?"

"No," we both answered in unison.

"Must I continually remind you to put others before you so you can more clearly see what it is that you should do before you do it?"

"Grandfather," I said. "It was one of the spirits of the land that told me to call you. Cheeway and I were doing just as you have instructed us to do by following their bidding."

I could see a look of surprise come over Grandfather's face when I told him that.

"Alright," Grandfather said, taking his hands off his hips and sitting down with the both of us. "Tell me what has happened that caused the both of you so much concern."

We spent the next hour explaining all of the events that had happened to both of us since the last time that he was with us on the land of the mesa where the two figures appeared to us. We did not leave any details out of the explanations and we could see that Grandfather had given both of us his complete attention. When we had finished our explanations to him, Grandfather simply lowered his head and nodded to us in an up and down manner and said, "I see what you needed me for. I regret not being there for the both of you. I feel that now would be a good time to explain some things that will help clear your minds on several aspects of my life path."

CHAPTER 5

❀

Path to the Right

"When I was a very young boy, I was much like the both of you," Grandfather began. "I, too, had a Grandfather who had taken great effort in explaining the balance of understanding the life path. It was during one of these lessons that the vision that we had seen together on the mesa had come to me for the first time.

"My Grandfather explained to me that this vision had come to me as a forewarning of things that were yet to be. He told me that my time to touch my other half spirit was close at hand and the spirits of the land were showing me the two who had made such a union in their life path.

"The two visions that we had seen lived many generations before and had long since passed their shells which held their spirits back to the Earth Mother. However, our people continue to carry their lessons in many of our song legends because of the great accomplishment that they have found.

"Their names are Two Elks and Morning Wind. What they represent to us is what could be, but unfortunately it does not come into existence for many that walk a life path with the Earth Mother.

"What Two Elks and Morning Wind show us is what could be if all is performed properly. These two spirits are the example that has been given to us by the Great Spirit, His lesson to us in what could be possible for all who share this life path with the Earth Mother. All of the blessings that are the Earth Mother's to give have been given to them. They show us a very valuable lesson, and it is one that I am sure that you will benefit from greatly.

"It was a time when our people lived in another land than the one that is located on the mesa. It was a time before much of our memory was considered necessary because in those days of our most ancient ancestors, time was not considered to be anything that would cause an end to a life path. We had been blessed greatly by the Earth Mother, the spirits of the land, and all of her children.

"It was a time when all of the spirits who came before her were very new to her domain and were still considered a great mystery to many of her children.

"The Earth Mother had given many blessings on all who would come to her to walk a life path. She had given more than ten times the number of years for the body to last as a walking vessel to the spirit; and for all of the time that the body would hold the spirit, there were no illnesses or bad moments in any of the life paths that were shared with her.

"All of the knowledge that was known by the spirit before entering the domain of the Earth Mother was retained. It was retained in a way that it had only to be sought after in a very easy manner. Even the knowledge that the spirit carries with it of the first separation from the Great Spirit was also made available, as well as the knowledge that we traveled through these many life paths with our own spirit families.

"However, in those days, the desires of the bodies became the leading force in almost all of the life paths that were being walked. In the time of only a few generations, the spirit was almost forgotten and the needs of the bodies were put in its place. It was the needs of the bodies that were pursued. The advancement of the spirit, which was the primary reason the Earth Mother ever allowed any of our spirits to visit with her in her domain, was forgotten.

"That is, it was forgotten by almost all of the spirits. There were a very few of them who continued to hold by the original intent of coming to the Earth Mother but they were regarded as outcasts and considered dangerous by all who would come into contact with them. In time, these others who were continuing to teach the way of the understanding of the balance of the life path were chased out of all of the lands where they tried to settle. However, that is a complete story in itself and not at all the one I wish to share with you at this time.

"The part of this history of our people that I wish to share with both of you is about Two Elks and Morning Wind. It is here that the lessons you will require will be learned."

Grandfather paused for a brief moment and looked up at the top of the sky that was beginning to put on its night colors for us to see.

"Look at what has been given to us," Grandfather said, as he continued looking up at the sky. "I wonder how many others who are walking a life path with us in these days will take a few moments out of their time to share in this beauty that is being shared with us from the Earth Mother.

"The Earth Mother is a very beautiful woman spirit and, as with all things, her beauty is only her reflection in the mirror to us. All that is in her could be in all of us. All that she gives to us is shared and what she wants in return is only to have us appreciate what she has given to us.

"She is not a selfish spirit. She only wants to give, but if her giving is ignored, then the time for the giving will be withdrawn. I wish that neither of you will have to encounter this withdrawal during the life path you are walking with her. I do not believe that either of you could be prepared for what this would mean. So now, let us admire the evening show that she is putting on for us."

For the next few moments, Cheeway, Grandfather, and I sat in silence and observed the many colors of the Earth Mother as she was dressing her children for the night. We could see that all of the land that was around us was becoming a reflection of the vivid colors she was showering over them and I could tell that by them reflecting her colors back to her, they were in actuality giving her praise for all of the wonderful blessings that she had bestowed on them during the period of the day that had just passed.

"It is late now and we must go to our homes," Grandfather said, as we could feel the peace that was filling the silence we had shared during this time.

"But what about the song legend you were sharing with us, Grandfather?" Cheeway asked, sitting on the back portions of his feet.

"This day is over now and as the Earth Mother has said her good night blessings to her children, I will also give each of you mine. Tomorrow will be another day and I will be by each of your houses very early. We will go back to the place on the mesa to continue the song legend of Two Elks and Morning Wind."

Both Cheeway and I knew that when Grandfather had made up his mind about what he would do, it would do neither of us any good to try to convince him otherwise. So, standing up, we all said our good night blessings to each other and went off in the directions of our own homes. We also knew that when Grandfather would tell us that he would be by our houses very early, that was exactly what he meant. And, since he had taken the time to tell us that he would come by early, if we were not ready to go with him, he would become upset with us and remind us of our lack of commitment for days after that.

The sleep spirit came to me very quickly that night and I was very thankful for it. I was prepared to wait and call to him for a long time because of the excitement that I was feeling by knowing that tomorrow Grandfather would continue his sharing of his speaking words to Cheeway and I about Two Elks and Morning Wind.

CHAPTER 6

❀

How Spirits Touch

Morning had come to our lands and I had gone outside to wait for Grandfather who said he would come and get me very early. I was looking to the east and could see that the life force from the new day was being announced by the wind spirit. Each morning, the wind spirit would go among all of the children of the Earth Mother and tell them of the upcoming events of the day and would carry all of the new messages from the Earth Mother for them to hear. It was in this way that there were no children sleeping when the new day would come to them.

This morning, I felt as if I were sharing this great event with all of her children. I could feel the wind spirit as it was crossing our lands informing the children they should be ready for it.

In this time, when it is neither day or night, Grandfather would always tell us that many secrets could be observed. The reason for this was that much like a child wakes up from a night's sleep, so do the children of the Earth Mother. They do not perceive anything around them except their natural self.

This morning, I could see one of the cats in the neighborhood playing with some small clumps of grass that were growing in the middle of the dirt path that went in front of our house. The small clumps of grass were being awakened by the wind spirit and the cat was reinforcing this message to them as well. It seemed like the cat realized that the small pieces of grass were not waking up as fast as they should have been and it was playing with them using its front paws to gently shake them back into their awake place so that they could meet the new morning.

I was becoming very involved with watching them help each other into the place they were supposed to be on this morning when the silence of the land was broken by the sounds of a loud motor coming down the dirt path. Looking up from the position I was standing. I could see that it was Grandfather's truck that was coming for me. In the front of the cab, I could see Cheeway, and by the way his head was resting on the back of the seat, I knew that he had found the dream spirit.

Not wanting to wake up any of the people who were still sleeping, I rushed out to the dirt path to meet Grandfather and his truck. He had seen me and stopped. I could see that Grandfather had shaken Cheeway awake and we busied ourselves in waving our farewells to my parents' house. We would do this so we would not make any of the spirits who were there feel left out of the adventure that we were about to begin.

Having finished our greetings and salutations, we turned the truck around and began to make our way out to the land of the mesa where Grandfather told us that he would continue his story about Two Elks and Morning Wind.

As we were traveling out to our destination, I turned my head in the direction where Cheeway was sitting. I could see that he was still communing with the sleep spirit and saw that his mouth was hanging open as it did so much of the time. I knew that if he were to leave it like this, by the time of our arrival on the mesa, that he would wake up with a mouth full of dirt from the roads that we were traveling. Feeling a little sorry for him, I reached over to his place in the seat and pushed his mouth closed with my hand.

Seeing that he was now buttoned up, I felt better and continued looking out of the window at our peoples' land of the mesa. I was thinking of all the adventures that had taken place here. Our people regarded the spiritual side of the life path with the greatest of respect and much of our teachings were centered around understanding these kinds of things. I was thinking how strange the others who were also walking a life path with the Earth Mother were for not being able to see the spiritual side of their life path. I was hoping that someday I might be able to share with them some of the things that I have learned so that they, too, could be able to understand the real meaning of what they had come here to do.

I caught Grandfather's face looking at me out of the corner of my eye and when I turned to look at him, he was smiling at me. Somehow, I felt that he had been reading me again without me knowing it. But from the smile he was sharing with me, I knew that he was only approving of the thoughts that were running through my mind as I was sitting in the truck with him.

We had reached our place on the land of the mesa after riding for about an hour and one half. I was not surprised to see that Cheeway had slept for the entire trip and we had to wake him up after Grandfather had stopped the truck and parked it behind a large rock that would provide it with its protection.

Grandfather had pointed our destination out to us and, picking up the provisions that he had brought, we began walking.

The air was very kind to us on this day because it was giving us a very gentle breeze. It was not unusual for this time of the year for the wind to blow very fiercely across our lands. If this had been the case, Grandfather would have had us both wrap up in our blankets before walking to the place he wanted to take us.

We had been walking for about an hour before we had come to the place where Grandfather stopped and told us that the place he wanted us to go was located on the top of a high cliff. We looked up at the side of the cliff. We did not see any way of climbing it.

Grandfather looked at both of us and placed both of his hands on his hips.

"You both have eyes but you have not yet learned to use them," Grandfather said to us, sharing a small smile that was crossing his face.

"If you will both look, you will see that there has been a great staircase chiseled into the entire stone face of this cliff."

Cheeway and I looked closely at the face of the cliff that was before us and above Grandfather's head. He was right, for just above his head, there were many holes that had been carved into the stone itself.

"What you are both looking at is how many of our ancestors would construct their stairways in order to climb up to the top of places they wished to get to. In time, you will be able to see these efforts more clearly but for now, I am satisfied to show you how to see what it is that you are looking at."

Having finished his speaking words to us, Grandfather began climbing up the face of the stone wall. We could see how both hands and feet would fit very well into each of the carved holes in the side of the wall and we followed.

When we were about halfway up the face of the cliff, we could feel the wind getting stronger and this concerned us greatly. If this was a calling of a needed storm by the children of the Earth Mother, we knew that it could very well push us all off of the side of this stone wall and the distance to the bottom was far enough to worry us.

"Do not concern yourselves with the spirit wind that is touching you. It means us no harm," came Grandfather's voice over the sound of the wind spirit's messages. "This wind spirit is only carrying messages to the children of the Earth Mother. It would appear as though some of the children have become confused with the time and were attempting to wake themselves up for the new growing season. The wind spirit is reminding them that it is still the sleeping season and if they were to wake up now, it would be very bad for them."

I was always very impressed with the quickness that Grandfather was able to interpret all things that would take place in his life path. I wanted to be like him when I, too, had as many seasons added to my life path.

We had reached the top of the mesa and I felt very accomplished with this since it was my first time at climbing it from the east side. Grandfather had already found a place where we would sit and it was not too far from the one we had sat on only a short time ago when we first saw the two images of Two Elks and Morning Wind.

"Once you have set our provisions up and we have made a suitable place for ourselves, I will continue with the story I began yesterday."

Hearing Grandfather's speaking words, Cheeway and I rushed about on this land in order to perform all that was required of us. Learning about our ancestors' histories was something that both Cheeway and I could listen to for days on end and we especially enjoyed hearing them from Grandfather.

Once we had accomplished our tasks and all of the things that we had brought with us were put in their proper place, we sat down and waited for the speaking words to begin.

"Grandfather," I said, in a very inquisitive tone of voice. "You told Cheeway and me that the reason that we saw the vision of Two Elks and Morning Wind was because we were about to meet our other half spirit. Did you mean that we were going to meet them soon?"

"I was mistaken about giving my speaking words too soon to both of you. What I should have said, if I had taken the time that I should have taken, was that both of you will be given the opportunity of passing them during your life paths."

"What does that mean, Grandfather?" Cheeway asked, sitting straight on his piece of ground that he had found.

"This means that both of you—and when I speak to each of you about your other half spirit, I am speaking of one of the spirits who are in our own spirit family—are walking a life path in this same time as you are. It also means that you both are very fortunate, because in most of the life paths this does not happen until we have crossed the great spirit waters and are in the waiting place."

"You mean that not all spirits who are walking a life path with the Earth Mother are able to meet their other half in the Earth Mother's domain?" I asked.

"This is the truth of what I have shared with both of you. It is the exception rather than the rule that the other half of your spirit is sharing the same time in the domain of the Earth Mother. However, this is a spirit that is from your own spirit family and they have come to walk a life path with the Earth Mother so that they may be joined with you when the time is right. It is also a rare occurrence to find a spirit that is prepared to meet their other half while they are both walking a life path with the Earth Mother."

"What happens if one of the spirits has not properly prepared themselves to meet this other half that you are talking about, Grandfather?" I asked, still sitting in a very attentive position on my piece of the mesa.

"It is as I have already told the both of you. When you have entered into a life path with the Earth Mother, the second split of the spirit family takes place. In very few cases will two spirits be placed here to be joined in the way that I will tell you of. Now, I am not aware of the reason for this, but I will say that if they are allowed to meet during their life path, there will be an unbounded joy that takes place in both of their lives.

"This is because they are of the same awareness and spiritual level. When they come together, it is a great combination of peace and harmony that will affect all who will come into contact with them. However, the two half spirits will not be allowed to know one another until all that was designed to be done by each of them has been completed. This is how they have decided if they would be able to meet in this life path. This is how they will have prepared themselves for meeting and recognizing each other.

"Now, you ask what would happen if neither of them would be prepared. If neither of them has accomplished all that they have set before themselves to perform and learn from, they would not recognize the other one for who they are. In every life path, there is much to do and understand. It is filled with great experiences that must be understood. In order for them to take their proper place in the life of the spirit, this understanding must be gained before anything else will follow.

"Unless this is accomplished, the spirit will not be recognized for what it is. This lack of recognizing is not only for the individual spirit, but it is for their other half as well."

"Grandfather," Cheeway asked. "What if only one of the half spirits was prepared? Could not only one of them recognize the other one for who they are?"

"This is not possible, Cheeway. You see, in order for one of them to attain that which they have set out to accomplish, the other one must be equally successful. Without both of them advancing their spirit, neither of them will find what it is that they are looking for.

"Think of it this way. Look at all of the people that each of you have come into contact with each day of your lives. Now, both of you are very young and because of the number of seasons that each of you have gone through is still small, the level of experiences that have happened to either of you has been very limited.

"Because of the limited experiences that each of you have gone through, your level of understanding is equally as limited. This creates a very shallow understanding of the life that each of you are on.

"Let us say, for the sake of argument, that you each have only accomplished one thing out of the thousands of things that you have set forth to do. At this very moment of time, I would not say that either of you are ready to cross over the great spirit waters to the waiting place because your levels of learning and understanding of the balance of the life path has not been attained.

"You see, when we have reached this level of understanding, it has been through much learning. This has come to us by living through many events that we can see the value of if we have learned to work through them. In all life paths, your spirit must put itself through many situations in order to grow. To many others who would attempt to look and judge each spirit from their perspective, it would seem that many of them are throwing away their life path because they hold these experiences they are going through as being too important. However, the real test for each of these spirits is not the level of acceptance or rejection that comes from others, it comes from the level of understanding that the spirit attains by working through these events that will come to them. This is where spiritual growth comes from. This is the knowledge and understanding that I am talking about to make a correct decision comes from.

"Each spirit that comes to walk a life path with the Earth Mother has set a specific time for themselves to accomplish all those things that they consider necessary for them to advance their spirit so that one day it may be able to rejoin with the Great Spirit. If they are able to accomplish this before the time that they have given to themselves, then they will be confronted by their spirit family and they will be given a choice of returning to the waiting place across the great spirit waters or remaining with the Earth Mother.

"These spirits have a very difficult decision to make. Because they have attained the level of understanding that was necessary to put them at the place they originally intended on being, and have met all of the conditions that have allowed their spirits to advance sufficiently, they realize what they are being offered by this choice.

"They have a very good understanding of the way they could live if they were to go back to the waiting place with the others of their spiritual family. They understand what pains and sorrows they will continue to encounter if they choose to stay with the Earth Mother for what remains of their time to walk a life path with her.

"However, because they have done all that they have come to the Earth Mother to do, those that decide to stay for the remainder of the time that has been allotted to them will accomplish great things. By accomplishing these things, they will not only advance their own spirits, but they will assist the entire spiritual family to which they are a part of to advance as well. It is from this point forward that they will receive help to accomplish the great quests that have been left to those who would do such a thing. They have come to the point where they have decided to remain in the Earth Mother's domain and undertake these great quests for her.

"Because they have completed all that they had set out to accomplish, they will be of sufficient understanding and wisdom to recognize their other spiritual half. They will be able to call them and the other half will have the understanding to hear them and come to them in this life path.

"When both halves of the spirit are joined, together they are capable of accomplishing feats that are greater than they have ever been capable of perceiving that they could accomplish. All who will come to know them, and all who will come to touch them, will feel this greatest of all gifts that they possess…a complete balance of union. All quests that they undertake will be successful and all of their successes will help others in seeing what it is that they must do in order to accomplish what they need to do. They become the guiding path for all who would have the eyes to see.

"This was the way of Two Elks and Morning Wind. They were the first of our people to attain this level of a life path. It is why we sing of them in so many of our song legends and it is why we will always revere them when they come to us.

"They come to us in many forms and shapes. The image of them that was presented to us on the land of the mesa was such a surprise to me that I could not think correctly for many days. I was trying to gather myself when the both of you interrupted me. However, because of what you both have told me of the events that led the both of you to do this, I understand more clearly now why you did what you did."

"Grandfather, could you tell us a little more about who Two Elks and Morning Wind were?" I asked, still sitting very attentively on my piece of ground that was before him.

CHAPTER 7

❀

Song Legend of Two Elks and Morning Wind

"Two Elks was a great hunter of our people. Because of his abilities and powers over all of the domain that was the Earth Mother's, he was given the ability to call on the spirits of the land. They would tell him of events that would happen to anyone long before they would happen. As our song legends of him tell us, he was well on his way to a position of great importance among our people. He had accomplished many things that assisted all who would come to him. He performed well in his service to others. Two Elks had achieved all that he had set out to perform during his life path with the Earth Mother.

"Having accomplished all that he had intended to perform, he was given the choice of returning to the waiting place by his spirit family. But he chose to remain with the Earth Mother until his time had run its course. Because of this decision, he became the one who would be the first of our people to find his other half spirit in these lands which are the Earth Mother's. His recognition had been advanced to a high place among our people. He was seen by many and one of those who had seen him was Morning Wind.

"Morning Wind did not have the same kind of life that Two Elks had. Hers was one that caused her to work through great pain and suffering and sorrow. She had known many braves in her younger times but she would not allow them to know her. She was a spirit who was very confused until this time when she saw Two Elks. Her life had been filled with much misery. She felt that if any others of our people ever knew what she had been through, they would not like her and throw her out of every village that she would go into.

"Before she knew Two Elks, this was her world. It was one of hiding herself from all others but always wanting to be accepted by someone who would be able to understand her. Because of this, Morning Wind had worked through all that had been set before her by telling herself that there would be someone someday who would be coming to her. When he would find her, he would be able to understand her and all that she had been through…they would be able to understand her pain and sorrow.

"Having accomplished all that she had set before herself to do while walking her life path with the Earth Mother, she was also given the choice of returning to the waiting place across the great spirit waters or remaining with the Earth Mother until the time that had been given to her was completed.

"For Morning Wind, this was a very difficult decision to make. Having gone through so much, she was thinking it would be a great blessing to be in a place where sorrow and pain were not known. However, her belief in the fact that there was one who was also walking a life path that would one day join her, she decided to stay with the Earth Mother and wait for him.

"Her choice was made only days before she had seen Two Elks. Because they both had accomplished that which they had set before themselves to do, when their eyes met in a great gathering of many of our people, they recognized each other for who they were. They knew that the other was the one they had been waiting for…now they would be together.

"In the beginning, their life was a complete surprise to many others who could not believe that Two Elks would put a woman before his duties and his people. However, what they did not see was that all of the duties that Two Elks was to perform were now being done with much more precision and accuracy. He did not require as much time to do them as he once did.

"As Two Elks became more and more efficient in the performance of his duties, there was a change that was coming over him. It seemed as if he could not go anywhere or do anything on his own. He was always seen with Morning Wind. This made some of the others, who had been used to having so much of his time to themselves, feel left out. They decided to find out more about Morning Wind.

"They did not have much difficulty in discovering the kind of life that Morning Wind had lived. They believed that they could use this to discredit both of them. Once this had been done, they believed that they would be able to step into the position that Two Elks had worked for. They believed that once the others would know about the past of Morning Wind, that they would force Two Elks out of his position.

"There were many seasons spent in planning the demise of Two Elks, and during this time Two Elks and Morning Wind were gaining great admiration by all they came into contact with. But those others, who were planning to discredit him through Morning Wind's past, were slowly slipping out of their power positions among our people.

"The day finally came when those others felt that they were ready to set the trap that they had put together so carefully over the past few seasons. They were going to tell all who had gathered before the two of them about the life that Morning Wind had been living before she had met Two Elks. They felt certain that when the others of our people would hear of her past, they would cast her out of all the villages and in the process of casting her out, Two Elks would leave with her.

"What they were hoping for was when Two Elks would leave that they would be able to enter his vacant position. However, for all of their planning, things did not turn out the way they had anticipated.

"Two Elks and Morning Wind had just finished addressing a large gathering of our people. They had been giving them instructions in the way of the spirit and how best to continue to advance it. In the middle of their speaking words, the spokesman for the group of the others saw his opportunity and rang out his speaking words so that all could hear.

"The speaker for the small group of others confronted not only Two Elks and Morning Wind with her past, but they also included all of those who had gathered near them as well. He spoke of all the other braves that Morning Wind had known in her past and how each of them was broken down to nothing more than a beggar.

"This speaker for the small group of others went into detail of how each of the braves she had met was very strong and virile. Because she did not return any of the love that they had offered to her, they began to shrivel up within themselves and slowly turn into nothing more than the shell which carried their spirits within it.

"This speaker stated that because of her past and all of the unspeakable things that she had done, that even she knew how bad her consequences had been. She knew that it was so bad, he continued, that she did not ever tell anyone of what her life was like in those seasons that were before she had come to Two Elks.

"This voice that was giving the speaking words to all who were gathered continued by saying that because she had been able to keep her beauty and the many other braves had been left with nothing, that she was using Two Elks in the same way that she had used the other braves. In a very short time, she would turn Two Elks into a worthless brave and lead him to become only a shadow of what he had once been.

"He continued by telling the others who were gathered around them that she would not only stop at Two Elks, but people like her would not ever be satisfied until she had been able to ruin their lives as well. He told them that the only reason she had been able to continue in her ways was because she took the spirit of life out of those she had come into contact with. When there was no more life in them, she would cast them away and look for another.

"All who were gathered before Two Elks and Morning Wind on that day fell silent and cast their eyes upon the two of them as they continued to stand before this gathering. However, there were no speaking words that were returned by either of them. Instead of addressing the speaker of the small group of the others, Two Elks took Morning Wind into his arms and held her close to him then walked away from those who were looking at them.

"Once Two Elks and Morning Wind had left them, the speaker of the small group of others continued to stick his untrue words into the minds and hearts of the others who were standing near to him. He told them all that now he had given them the truth of what their future would have been like if they had allowed the two of them to stay in their respected positions of power, that they should spread this new found knowledge among the rest of the people and see if they would be contented to leave Two Elks and Morning Wind in these positions.

"He reminded them that they were headed for certain destruction if they did not take all status and positions away from the both of them. He then offered himself as a temporary substitute for the positions that they should make vacant. He told them that he would do his best to reverse all of the trends that Morning Wind had begun. But to correct what damage there was among all of them, he would need to have much assistance from those he knew would perform in their best interest.

"He told all who were gathered before him now where they would be able to find those many other braves so they could see for themselves what empty shells that Morning Wind had left of them. He suggested to all of them to go and see for themselves what had happened to these braves Morning Wind had robbed of life because this was what could have happened to them had it not been for him. When they would return, they would be able to make up their own minds about what they should do about Two Elks and Morning Wind and the position that was soon to be vacant.

"In the many days and nights that followed the initial confrontation, the following of the small group grew. Many had gone to see for themselves what these once proud braves had been turned into and returning to the site where the speaker said he would meet them, they numbered many.

"The speaker stood before the large gathering and asked what should become of him and his more than generous offer of taking the place of Two Elks and Morning Wind. The others who were gathered before him said in unison that he should take over the place where Two Elks and Morning Wind once filled and that whatever it would require for him to correct any of the possible damage that they had done to them. He had their permission to follow his own path to do so, but it must be started very quickly.

"That was all the speaker needed to satisfy his plans. He informed all who had gathered before him that within two days, he would come up with a plan and name all who would be needed by him to serve them. During all of this time, neither Two Elks nor Morning Wind had been seen. Because of all the confusion that had been created by the speaker, no one had even thought of them.

"The two days had passed and as the speaker promised, he had gathered them before him. He let them know what he had intended to do about any possible damage that may have been caused by Two Elks and Morning Wind. He informed them that he had chosen many others who would be working with him. Because of the size of this task to not only correct any damage that had been done, but to ensure that there would be no lasting effects, his group would not be able to perform any of the work that was required to sustain themselves. Their sustaining would have to be provided by the others whom they were protecting and the way that this would be accomplished would be rather a simple one.

"He informed these others that they would be required to give him one in ten of all that they would produce. This, he told them would ensure that his group would be able to continue their guard against any of the evil that had been created by Two Elks and Morning Wind. He reminded them that if they did not do this, they would not be able to conduct the necessary functions that would ensure their safety from all of the evil that they had been exposed to.

"When he was asked by some of those who were gathered around him how long this would take, the speaker only smiled at them and told them that it would take as long as it would take.

"The others were not happy with this but the speaker told them that neither Two Elks nor Morning Wind had been seen and he believed that they were performing great magic to make all of them pay for what they had done to them. He scared all of those who were gathered before him and because of this fear, they consented to pay for the services and protection that the speaker said he would give to them.

"In the many seasons that followed, the speaker and his group became very wealthy and the gathering of others who had listened to him became very poor. In more seasons, it was the speaker and his group who had all of the wealth while all of those who had listened to them were left with nothing.

"It had been many seasons since even speaking words that would tell of Two Elks and Morning Wind and been spoken by anyone. Even their memory of all that had been done by them was almost forgotten until one morning in the center of their village that it happened.

"It was customary for all of the people to gather on a certain day of the season in the center of the village. They would bring that which they all agreed to pay the speaker and his group. As they had met, they saw the speaker and many of his following coming down the path. They had all gathered to pay what they could for another season of protection.

"Just as the speaker and his group had entered the place that had been designated for them to collect their payment, one of the villagers shouted that there were two others who were coming into their village and they seemed to be bringing sunshine with them.

"The first thought that had crossed the speaker's mind was that there would soon be two others from whom he would be able to collect more payment. As he looked at the two who were walking into the village, he could only see that one of them was a man and the other one was a woman. Neither he, nor any of the others who had been gathered before him could see anything more. Both of these people had their entire heads and bodies covered with a hooded blanket.

"As they walked into the village, the speaker called their attention to himself and his group of followers. He told them what he would require of them so that he and his group could provide them with the protection that they would need from the great evil magic that had been performed by Two Elks and Morning Wind.

"Just as the speaker finished his speaking words to them, they stopped where they were and looked around the entire group that had been gathered before them. Glancing over the group only once they both reached for the top of their hooded blankets together and pulled them off from themselves.

"As their covering fell away, a strange silence fell over the entire group. For what they saw in front of them was Two Elks and Morning Wind. What was even more amazing was the fact that they had not aged even one day from the many seasons that they had been away.

"Standing in silence before all who had gathered before them, Two Elks took Morning Wind into his arms and they embraced warmly so that all could see that the love that they had once shared with all who could see was still there. As they embraced each other there was a beautiful flute melody that accompanied them and in the far distance all could hear the beating of two drums that they could tell represented their two lovers' hearts.

"Seeing this, all of the villagers knew immediately what they had done was wrong and began to walk toward Two Elks and Morning Wind so that they could receive their forgiveness. However, as they began to walk to their position, both of them vanished. Just as they vanished, so did the beautiful music that had been playing for them while the two of them were caught in each other's embrace.

"The speaker and his entire group were very upset about this appearance of Two Elks and Morning Wind. One of the villagers overheard one of the speaker's followers say to him that he thought that they had been killed on the day that he had told the others of the past life of Morning Wind.

"That was all that the group who had been paying so dearly for their protection needed to hear to raise their anger against all of them. In unison, the villagers rushed the speaker and his group and ended their life path with the Earth Mother.

"However, now they had no one at all. They had cast out Two Elks and Morning Wind and had now finished the life path of the one they had paid their money to for so many years. They all thought that they would perish because for the first time in their life paths, they were without leadership.

"Just as they were about to enter the dark side of their despair, they heard the same flute and drum music come to them once again. As it reached their ears, it also touched on their hearts and spirits. There was a veil that was lifted from their life path and all that was needed to be seen, could now be seen and understood by all.

"Once again, their eyes, hearts, and spirits were opened to themselves. They all knew that it was because of the goodness of those who had once been Two Elks and Morning Wind. Even now that they were spirits, the love that they had for them was great enough to call them back to the villagers from across the great spirit waters and the waiting place. They returned to them to remind them of the truth that was embedded in the understanding of the balance of the life path which they were walking. It was to remind them what would bring about the advancement of their spirit and that this was the most important reason for them to be here.

"The villagers continued to see Two Elks and Morning Wind. Over the length of time that our people have been walking the life path with the Earth Mother, they have always made their presence known to our people in their times of great need. The goodness that is them reminds us all of the love that they found within themselves and the love that they still have for all of our people. When they make their appearance known to us, we know that this is a sign that great and good things will come to all who will be able to see them.

"This is how Two Elks and Morning Wind have been put into our song legends. Have I explained well enough for the both of you to understand?" Grandfather said, as he was looking over to the horizon where our lands could be seen extending to the place where they would meet the sky.

"Grandfather," I said, as I continued to look in his direction, "you told Cheeway and I that we have seen Two Elks and Morning Wind because our other half spirit was also walking a life path with the Earth Mother. But you saw them as well. Does this mean that you have a half spirit walking a life path as well?"

CHAPTER 8

❀

I Bent My Heart

"I have already met my half spirit, but she is no longer walking a life path with the Earth Mother. Both of you knew her as the woman I had taken for my wife."

We could see that sharing these speaking words with us was becoming very difficult for Grandfather. When we looked closely at him, we could see that there were small water wells that were building up within his eyes. After thinking about the speaking words that he had shared with both of us, he turned his attention to both of us and continued.

"When I was also a young man on our lands, I was visited by the spirits of Two Elks and Morning Wind. My grandfather explained to me what this vision meant for me and I became very excited about the possibility of finding my other half spirit walking a life path with the Earth Mother.

"My grandfather had always told me that the balance of the life path told him that only the ones who would have a half spirit and would meet them, would only do so when they had finished all that they had set out for themselves to do.

"I became very intent on preparing myself for this meeting. I would examine all possibilities that would come to me so I could glean my learning from them. In this way, I was sure that I was attaining the needed level of understanding that was necessary for me to be able to recognize my half spirit when the time would come.

"Just as I have told both of you, my Grandfather told me the same things. The most important thing that kept running through my mind was the fact that our paths would one day cross and I wanted very much to be prepared to recognize her when they did. My Grandfather also told me that if one of us was not prepared to meet the other one, that when the time would come for both of us to cross our paths, we would both cross as mere acquaintances and nothing more.

"As it happened, we were both prepared and when we finally met, it was more than obvious. The feeling and the day are still as fresh in my mind now as they were when it happened. You see, when we met, our spirits touched and once this connection was made, everything else fell into place.

"Both of us not only felt the similar physical affection for each other, but everything that we would discover and do together had a feeling with it that we had done these things many times before. This sense of familiarity helped us both to grow and because of this growing, we soon found that we made one complete person and one complete spirit.

"As we continued to grow, each time that we would work through another of life's problems together, I could hear the same music that always accompanied Two Elks and Morning Wind whenever they would come among our people. Because of this repeated occurrence, I could tell that the song legends that hold both of them in it were not mere stories that we tell our children. They were our history of true events that we could still see if we would only take the time to look for them.

"We both discovered that all of the things that we each had gone through and worked through in our life paths alone were for a definite reason. This reason prepared each of us for the other. The strengths that I brought to her, she needed to make up for the weaknesses that she had not been able to develop on her own. The strengths that she brought to me were needed by me in order to make up for the weaknesses that I was not able to develop on my own.

"We found a great sense of peace and security in being with each other and we also found that as we continued to walk our life path, each day would bring us closer and closer to each other. Soon, there was no longer a me or a her, but in those places, there was a we. It was this we state of development that we discovered that each of us was making a place in the other one's life. Because this was happening in such a peaceful and joyful way, we did not mind and because this was happening to both of us, we were able to relate to it very well."

Grandfather paused to let his memories catch up to him. I could see that a very warm smile had formed over his face. The way Grandfather looked on that day with the morning sun shining on his white hair and crinkled face that was holding a smile reminded me of a time in our people's history when we were free and were not held by any fences or borders. Looking at Grandfather on this morning and in his story, I had been able to create a lasting picture of him and the peace that was rolling over him.

"Did you have to go far to find your other half spirit?" Cheeway asked, still sitting on the edge of his feet.

"I did not have to go any further than the village I had grown up in, Cheeway," Grandfather answered, still wearing the same peaceful smile on his face.

"We had been together all of the time that we were walking a life path. But because neither of us was ready yet, we did not recognize the other one for who they were.

"Let me get back to the place that I was telling the both of you about because it will be very important to you as you continue to pass more seasons on the life path you are walking.

"We had been growing so close together that we did not notice just how much of our time was being shared with the other one. Our friends would often ask us both if we did not ever tire of the other one and need a little time to ourselves. But we would always answer them that whatever we would do or wherever we would go, it was just so much more comfortable to go and do all of these things together.

"In time, we were able to be with the other one even when we were not together. By this time, we had become so much a part of the other one's life that we would carry the other one with us. I do not mean that all of them would be with the other one, what I do mean is this.

"As I have told each of you, we each came to the other one with strengths and weaknesses. Our strengths, that we had developed over the time we had walked our life path without the other one, matched the corresponding weaknesses the other one came into the union with. It was in this way that we had joined as one person and as one spirit. What we had developed within ourselves would be exactly what the other one needed to assist in their development of their spirit.

"As we both had sufficient time to grow and depend on the other one, when the inevitable times would come for each of us to have to conduct our tribal duties without the other one, we would give our weaknesses over to the other one for safekeeping. In this way, we both knew that whatever would happen to either of us that it would be the combined strengths of both of us that would continue to strengthen ourselves and our union. We also discovered that when we would return to the other one, that those same weaknesses that we had given over to the other one would always come back to us, but they had more strength and understanding in them than they did when we first gave them over."

Once again, Grandfather paused and he looked at each of us with a very intent but sad look on his face.

"If it was not for each of us being able to hold a part of the other one within us, I do not believe that we would be having this conversation on this day."

"What do you mean, Grandfather?" I said, trying to help him bring out the speaking words that we both felt were necessary for him to share with us.

"When my wife's time came for her to finally pass across the great spirit waters to the waiting place, I felt as if I was going to go insane with the mourning of her loss. I had not realized just how empty my life was without her to comfort me with her love and caring until she had left.

"We had filled such a great place in each of our lives that while she was still here with me, I did not notice how great her place was. However, when she passed over to the waiting place, that was when the sudden awareness came over me. Had it not been for the ability of keeping her with me and understanding who it was that would come to me every day and night, I would not have been able to recognize her for who she was in her spirit form. She was still giving me her love and caring. If I had not been able to recognize her, I do not believe that I could have been able to stay behind and perform what I was given to do by the others who had come to visit me."

CHAPTER 9

❀

A Healing Vision

"So the reason that you stayed behind and did not follow her across the great spirit waters was because you were given a task to accomplish?" I asked. "Was this task given to you by the spirits of the land, Grandfather?"

"Indirectly it was," he replied. "However, the ones who came to me on the night my wife passed over to the waiting place were the ones who have been coming to our people for as long as we have had song legends.

"They have come to us from all directions in our people's history and are always associated with Two Elks and Morning Wind. They come in the form of hooded men and none have ever seen their faces, but from every account that has come from our people, they have not ever changed their appearances nor the methods they have used in helping us.

"It was early on the first evening that grandmother had passed over to the waiting place. I heard the familiar sounds of the flutes and drums playing from the top of the mesa that was just behind our house. I did not believe these sounds at first but as time continued, I heard them come to me in such a loud voice that I could not ignore them any longer. I walked out of my house to see where they were coming from.

"As I walked out of the house, I could see that it was almost the in-between time where the day meets the night and many of those spirits who are coming to help us live. I looked up at the top of the mesa that was behind my house and saw them. I could tell even from the far distance that it was Two Elks and Morning Wind standing on the top of the mesa. As the fading sunlight was giving them their form, I could see that they were holding each other and looking down at where I was standing.

"In unison, they raised their outside hands toward me and then pointed back to the inside of my house. I could tell that they wanted me to return to the inside and without hesitating, I immediately turned around and went back inside.

"Just as I entered through the door, I saw that there were three others waiting for me. I recognized them as the ones who were in so many of our song legends and knew that they would bring no harm to me.

"For the entire day, before I had seen the vision of Two Elks and Morning Wind, I had been asking our ancestors for their permission to return across the great spirit waters and join my wife. However, for the entire day, I was receiving no answers from any of them. I was beginning to think that I had truly been left alone until I heard the music of Two Elks and Morning Wind. Then I knew that my requests had been answered and when I had walked out of the house, I had fully expected to be taken away by one of the in-between spirit riders who would carry me away with him. I expected to be with my wife once again.

"Now, standing on the inside of my house, I was looking at three of the ones who had given so much help to all of our people. It was then that I knew that I would be given another choice. It would be a choice that would allow all who were a part of our spirit family to advance their spirits. I knew that it would be a choice that I would wish to accept.

"I will tell you more about them later, but for now let me continue with the ending of this story that I have begun for both of you.

When I walked into the house, there the three of them stood. They stood there in silence but I could feel them walking around on the inside of me. In their hands, they each held a picture and when they were sure that I had seen that they each had something to show me, they each held out the picture that they were holding and pointed to me in a way that I could not misinterpret their meaning. They wanted me to look at the ones who were in the pictures.

"I looked at them. I saw that they had one picture of me and one picture of each of you. Then, and without any prompting, the middle one used the old hand language of our people to tell me what it was they wanted me to accept as a new task for what time remained for me in this life path.

"Their request of me was that I stay for the remainder of the time that had been allotted to me by the Earth Mother. The reason that I was to stay in the

Earth Mother's domain was to be able to instruct the both of you in the ways of understanding of the balance of the life path.

"They told me that the times ahead for both of you were going to be filled with many possibilities and what both of you would be capable of doing, with the assistance of myself, would benefit all who would ever come to walk a life path with the Earth Mother.

"They also told me many things that would come over the Earth Mother's domain. They gave me a date and a time when there would come a devastation to all of the Earth Mother's domain and many would suffer greatly. They told me of things that I have not been given permission to speak of to any and some that I was to pass on to only the two of you.

"One of these things that I have been given permission to tell the both of you is that I will be given the time to instruct the both of you. Each of you will be given the opportunity of assisting the Earth Mother, the spirits of the land, and her children, to provide help to many other spirits if you both choose to take up the quest that will be presented to you.

"It was because of this task that I chose to remain with the Earth Mother until my time had been completed. I could understand what it was that they were telling me and as they continued to share the hand language with me, my level of understanding was increasing by the moment. At the end of the conversation that was taking place on this night, I felt my mind and spirit had advanced greatly because of all that was shared with me and what was planned for the both of you. I could feel my importance grow within myself as I took up this quest that had been given to me. I know, in the times when each of you has lived through enough seasons, that the both of you will feel this same level of understanding and direction as I now have.

"It was on that same night that the three visitors who had come to me reassured me of my wife's presence with me. The middle one produced another picture of her. As he held it out to me, I could feel her presence. As I felt her come to me on this night, I closed my eyes and made a picture of her so that from that time on, I could have her new face and body and would be able to recognize it whenever she would give me her assistance."

Grandfather looked slowly at us then looked up at the brilliance of the blue that was in the sky above us and said, "From that time, she has not ever left my side and she wants me to tell the both of you that she is and will be very proud of all the things that each of you will be able to accomplish while you are walking your life path with the Earth Mother.

"After this, I opened my eyes to look at the three visitors once again but when I had opened them, they were gone. There was not even the smallest of traces that they had ever been there except for one thing. As I looked at the floor where the three of them had been standing, there and in the same order that they had shown them to me were the four pictures that they had used to tell me of things that were yet to come. Behind each of these pictures there was writing on them…it said, 'You are not alone.'"

Grandfather had finished sharing his speaking words with us and remained silent while looking at the both of us.

"Grandfather," I said, in a rather concerned tone of voice, "you said that there would be terrible things that would take place within the domain of the Earth Mother. Will there be any signs that we might be able to see that will give us a warning of when these times are coming close?"

"Yes, there will be many signs and I will give you some of them later. However, for the time being, I wish to take both of you to a very old village that has long been returned to the Earth Mother and tell you what had happened there. I believe that this place will give the both of you great strength when the times come for you to need it."

PART III

A CALL FROM THE WIND

CHAPTER 10

⊛

The Village of Empty Shadows

Grandfather got up from his sitting position and began walking toward a place that was on the mesa that neither Cheeway nor myself had ever gone to before. I asked him why he had not ever taken either of us to this place before. Grandfather stopped in his position and looked at the both of us and said, "Before now, there was no reason to." Then he continued walking.

Both Cheeway and I knew that to try and question Grandfather further on this matter was not going to benefit anyone because once he had made up his mind on what he was willing to share with us, there was nothing further that either of us would be able to do.

We walked in the direction that was away from the sun for about two and one half hours and then Grandfather suddenly stopped and looked straight ahead. Cheeway and I had been busy looking at the surrounding land that we were walking on and had become preoccupied in some of the carvings and stone drawings that were on some of the stone faces. We had become so intent on looking at all of them that we did not see Grandfather stop which resulted in both of us running into him.

"It is very good to see that you are both using your eyes and ears to become so aware of all that is going on next to you. I only hope that my body will last through this learning stage that both of you seem to be in," Grandfather said to us, as he was repositioning himself where he was once standing.

"We are sorry for running into you, Grandfather," we both said, as we bent our heads to look at the ground. We were feeling very bad about running into him and with so much force that it nearly toppled him over.

"Well, now that this has been settled, I would like both of you to look at the valley that is below us and tell me what it is that you see."

Cheeway and I looked over the valley below us and saw that there was nothing to see. This confused us both and we told Grandfather that we did not find anything there that would tell us otherwise.

"This is true," Grandfather said, as he continued to look into the valley that was before us.

"Then why did you ask us to look for something, Grandfather?" I asked, sounding very puzzled.

"What you see before you is all that remains when the spirit of life leaves a place. What you see before you will be what remains of all life as you perceive it once you have returned across the great spirit waters to the waiting place.

"I wanted to bring both of you here because of what has happened to our people who lived here long ago. There is a very important lesson that can be realized by the mistakes that have been made on this land. I believe that while this lesson may not be understood by either of you now, in the time that you each have left in the life path that you are walking, you will need this information in order to accomplish many of the quests that you will be called on to do. Let us find a place to sit on the sand and I will tell you both of the time when many promises were made. It was a time when such promises were made but they were not done in a way that would bring them to a lasting life."

We three sat down by one of the large stones that were on the hill side. Once we had made ourselves comfortable, Grandfather continued sharing his speaking words with us.

"In the process of preparing yourselves to meet your other half spirit, there will be many things that both of you will be required to do. As both of you will come into one quest after another, you will reach many high and low places in your time that you will spend with the Earth Mother.

"Both of you understand some of the things that you have been taught by our way of life. The one that I will talk to you about now and in this place is the one that speaks of a person being as good as their word that they give.

"I want to take this time to tell both of you that this statement that we live by is very true. However, there are many things that must be understood first before it can become your way of life.

"Before I was ready to meet your grandmother, I was a young man who was always in search for the hidden knowledge of the ways of our people. I would spend many days and nights roaming the places where we once lived. I considered myself to be very knowledgeable of the things that I had been able to accomplish. But as both of you will feel when this time comes for each of you, there was always something that seemed to be missing.

"In my own way of thinking, I believed this thing that was missing in my life that would be able to give me the feeling of accomplishment was in my direction and commitment to doing things as I would have them done. I believed that what I needed to do was to set goals for myself and make them always relate to the others that were around me.

"In the beginning, I was able to achieve a little of this but I wish to tell both of you that it was only a little. Each time that I would find new or discover old knowledge, I would bring this information back to the wise ones of our village in hopes of seeing them exalt me to the very top of our people for having accomplished a great thing.

"However, what I soon discovered was that while the information and knowledge that I brought to them was appreciated, I did not feel as though any of them regarded me as the one who had made such a great contribution to our people. I could not understand this new feeling that I was receiving and would continue to make additional discoveries in hopes of finding the one that would put me in the place where I wanted to be.

"It was during this quest for the ultimate piece of information that would give me the fame and recognition that I was looking for that led me to this land that we are sitting on now.

"In my process of looking for another source of information, I had quite accidentally come to this land that we are sitting on. I had been led here by some kind of a helping hand. But I did not know, nor did I wish to take the time of trying to understand, what it was that was guiding me. I was only interested in finding the things that would allow me to be raised to a higher level of respect and recognition among the people of our village.

"I told both of you to look out to the valley that is before us to see if there was anything that you could see. Both of you told me that there was nothing that you could see. Well, there is a great truth in your saying that, because this is what I saw as well.

"As I stood in this very same position those many seasons ago, there came a great wind over the land where I was standing. It was so strong that I had to cover myself in my walking blanket just to keep the sand and dirt out of my eyes. However, when the great wind was over and I pulled my head out of the walking blanket that I had been wrapped up in, I saw that there was an opening in the face of this rock that I had been standing close to.

"It did not dawn on me at the time, but later as I thought about it, the wind that had come suddenly over our land in this place where I was standing had arrived and left without any warning. It had come with only one purpose in mind…and that was to show me this opening that was located on the side of the large stone that I was standing next to. Later, I came to understand that this same wind spirit was also the one who was guiding me to this place. I know now that this journey that I had made was my final preparation in getting ready to meet my other half spirit, the one who would become your grandmother.

"I walked into the opening of the stone structure and found that I needed to go back to my truck and get my torch and some rope so I would be able to see where I was going. I used the rope to mark my way along the passages that I was going to travel. There were many possibilities that I could travel and they began within a few feet after entering the cave that had been opened up to me.

"As I walked to a place where the cave traveled into several directions, I stood there trying to decide which direction I would take. I felt the same force come over me once again that had led me to this land. This time, I did not resist it but went with it willingly.

"I rounded many curves that were in the cave and each time that I would round another, I was receiving a stronger and stronger feeling within me. It was the kind of a feeling that I knew what I would find at the end of this journey. I continued going forward, and as I did the force that was guiding me at first was now pulling on me to hurry up.

"I felt as though I had been traveling in this dark cave for almost an hour when I saw a light shine up ahead of me. For a brief moment I paused to try to adjust to this new turn of events that had come to me but the force that had brought me here would not allow me to stay for very long and after a few short moments, I was going forward once again.

"As I continued with my forward movement, I could see that the light was getting bigger. This was a very strange occurrence I was thinking. In the depth of this cave, I did not believe that there would be any way possible for the light from above to reach here, even through cracks or holes that would have been in the ceiling rocks. However, I did not receive any bad feelings or apprehensions about it, so I continued on with my journey.

"As I continued into the direction of the light, I felt the pushing from the same force that had guided me to this place suddenly stop. When it stopped, so did I. I just stood where I was and looked at the light that was shining in front of me. I could see that it was not the kind of light that would be made from the sun, but it was a created light. I could not tell where its source was coming from, but as I studied it, it maintained the same size and location.

"Since I could see nothing beyond the light, I decided that it was time for me to leave this place. I did not want to waste any time in a place where there was nothing for me to discover. Just as I turned around to head back in the direction that I had come from, I heard a voice come to me and it said, 'You would do me a great honor to come and sit with me for awhile.'

"I turned around to the direction where the voice had come from. As I turned around, I saw an old man sitting in the middle of the lighted area. I was very surprised to see him sitting there because just a few moments before there was no one there, and I did not hear anyone approach.

"'Who are you?' I asked, standing perfectly still in the place where I was.

"'I am called Wind From The East,' came the voice back to me.

"'Are you lost? Do you need my assistance to find your way out of this cave?'

"'Thank you very much for your concern, but I am very comfortable where I am. As for being lost, I do not believe that I am as lost as you are.'

"'Come and sit with me and I will tell you what you have been seeking.'

"I walked over to the place where Wind From The East was sitting and made a place for myself. I did not know this old man, but he seemed to know me. He not only told me what my name was but he told me who all of my ancestors were as well.

"After getting over my initial shock of his most complete display of knowledge, I asked him how he knew so much about me when I had not even seen him in any of our villages.

"'I have been among your people for a great amount of time. I have also visited those who would come to me in search of guidance and wisdom so that they may better understand the balance of the understanding of the life path that they are on.

"'I know this also about you, young man. You have spent much time gathering so much information and uncovering many of the secrets of your people in hopes of attaining a standing among them. Have you attained that which you have been seeking?'

"I could only look at Wind From The East and sadly shake my head in a left to right direction which would tell him that I had not been successful.

"'Well then,' Wind From The East said, 'perhaps you have been looking in the wrong directions. I believe that the places that you have been looking have all been traveled before. This only results in you rediscovering that which has been discovered before.

"'I believe that you have been trying to achieve things that you could not hold onto anyway. Your efforts have all been in producing things from the past in hopes that others in your village would give you a high place. However, to the ones who have attained the true wisdom of walking a life path with the Earth Mother, this is not very important. All knowledge that has ever been is and will always be available to those who know how to call on it.

"'The direction that your quest lies is within yourself. Not in the ways that have been walked many times before. In order to achieve that which you seek, you must stop trying to produce many things for others to look at. You must increase the inner understanding that will release the spirit that is within you. If you do this, you will find that what you desire most in life will be released to you. You will be able to see that it has always been with you. You do not need to waste your time in chasing after the shadows of things that will not ever bring you what you seek. Spend your time wisely and look within. No matter what you will try to create in this life path that you are walking, it will not ever out-live you. And when you reach the waiting place across the great spirit waters, you will see how futile all of your efforts have been. This will cause you great sadness because you will see what you should have been trying to achieve and I tell you that what you are doing now is not it.

"'Tell me something, young man, did you see any great buildings or monuments that were on the outside of this cave?'

"'No, I did not see anything that I could be able to call by those names.'

"'What did you see in the lands that are beyond the opening to this cave then?'

"'There is nothing but the balance of rocks and sand that the Earth Mother has created for her children who live here.'

"'Would you believe that once there was a great village that thrived on this place not more than ten generations ago and that they spent more than thirty of their years in building many great statues to honor a great event that had been given to them?

"'However, the reason that there is no trace of there ever being a village or monument there is that what was given to them was accepted by those who lived there but it was accepted for the wrong reasons. Instead of seeing the wisdom of the gift, they spent all of their time in trying to pay homage for what had been given to them and in hopes of getting more.'

"I could tell that Wind From The East was about to tell me this story, so I leaned back against the side of the cave wall and prepared myself to listen to the speaking words he was going to share with me.

"'It was a time when the Spaniards were still new to this part of the country and our people were the prominent culture. It was somewhere in the early sixteen hundreds and communications lines between villages were from small to non-existent. The village was physically located just outside the opening of the cave and spread out across the valley that is still there. The village was populated by about five hundred and fifty people of whom only about three in ten percent were not Indian. The inhabitants of the village were mostly farmers but a few of them did own a trading store or two and would provide the other villagers with those things they could not grow or produce for themselves. The Indians in the area enjoyed remarkable health and had told the Spaniards of those who would walk about giving them back their health when they were sick. At that time, the Spaniards merely shed this off as just another of the Indian's legends that had no meaning.

"'After the Spaniards had been in this area for about two years, there was an outbreak of a disease similar to cholera for which there was no cure. The disease was not selective as to race or age and was spreading very quickly to the entire population. The people there were convinced that it would eventually spread to everyone and there would be no one left alive to tell of their village. After the first few days, more than ten people had died and the villagers had taken their bodies to a place far from their dwellings to burn them.

"'All the Spaniards who shared the village with the Indians had heard of two spirits that the Indians called Two Elks and Morning Wind. The heard the Indians calling to them to ask for their intervention. When they asked the Indians who they were calling to, they told them the story of how they had always come to them in their times of need and let it go at that. As the illness of the village reached greater levels and they saw more of their friends and acquaintances die from it, the Spaniards joined the Indians in their morning and evening calls to those called Two Elks and Morning Wind. They were desperate for help of any kind…and prepared to receive the assistance that they were asking for.

"'On their way back to the village from burning more of their friends who had passed over the great spirit waters, they heard the sounds of flutes and drums being played in the distance. As they looked over in the direction of one of the hills that was overlooking their village, they saw two figures standing and holding each other. Just in front of them, they saw three other figures calmly walking over the hills and toward the village. Since they seemed to be heading in the direction of their village, they wanted to warn them that the village was filled with sickness and they should not enter at this time.

"'As they walked closer to the three individuals, they could see that they were dressed in long robes with hoods over their faces and leather sandals on their feet. At first they thought they were either Franciscan or Benedictine monks, but none of the villagers could recall any church or monastery in their area that could send three travelers out without any supplies or water. Another thing that was puzzling them was the fact that the closer they came to them, the louder the flute and drums were getting.

"'The land was still scarcely inhabited and that meant if a traveler were to go off in any direction, especially without water, it would bring disaster to their travels. As the villagers approached the three individuals, they were surprised to see that while the robes looked like the ones the monks would wear, the color was different and the material seemed to be lighter in texture and changed colors as the sun hit it from different directions. There was also concern because the three individuals did not ever look up so the villagers could see their faces. They maintained a posture of having their hooded faces facing toward the ground which kept their faces hidden.

"'When one of the villagers hailed the group of three with his warning, there was no response but the three continued on in the direction of the village without stopping or hesitating one step of the way. Those who were left inside the village heard the warning and came out to see what it was all about and saw the group of three coming in their direction.

"'Once inside the village, the three travelers individually walked into each house and shop where there was illness and simply touched the infected ones at various places on their bodies without any exchange of words between them. They continued this until every inhabitant and every building in the village had been visited. Once this was completed, they grouped together again and began to walk in the opposite direction they had entered, pausing only to touch that same group of villagers that had followed them into the town at the beginning.

"'One of them walked through the group and paused only at one of the villagers. This was the only person who had been complaining of not feeling well that day, and was touched on the head, arms and shoulders for a brief moment. The individual then turned back to the other two and they continued on their journey out of the village and back over the hills where they had come from. The villagers watched them as they walked out of the village and eventually passed out of sight over the hills that surrounded them. Looking up to the hills that were above them, they saw that the two who had been standing and observing while holding each other also turned and walked away. As all finally vanished from their sight, the flute and drum sounds passed just as quietly.

"'There was a long pause in the sounds that normally accompany life's daily routine and some of the villagers believed that they were already dead and in the afterlife. Suddenly, the silence was broken by a woman crying and weeping from the inside of her small adobe hut. The villagers, who had just stood out in the street during this whole process, ran into the hut to see a woman bent over her six month old baby crying. Thinking that the baby was dead, they proceeded to where the woman was in an effort of putting the small body on their handcart to carry it off and burn the body. However, when one of the men reached down to lift the mother's head off of the baby, they were surprised to see that the infant was very much alive and on top of that, all of the sickness spots on its body were gone. They discovered that the mother was crying out of joy and not out of anguish.

"'The woman was beaming an explanation to those villagers of what had transpired in her small hut. There was a man, or at least she thought it was a man, dressed like a priest who walked into her house and sat down next to her and her sick infant. She did not ever look closely at him because all of her attention and concern was focused on her infant who she believed to be very near death. She remembered seeing his hand caress the infant's head, arms, and shoulders and her infant responding with a sigh of relief. After that, the individual simply stood up and left her hut without ever uttering a sound or a word. She sat there and just stared at her young baby. She noticed that gradually he was showing more and more signs of life. She sat and stared at this in amazement and when he opened his eyes and looked at her and yawned, she could do nothing but cry from joy. It seemed the more she thought of how wonderful this thing had been, she would begin to cry more until she recognized the presence of those villagers, who came into her hut and gently pulled at her.

"'Some of the Indian residents, who had also been affected with this disease and were cured did not have as difficult a time as did the Spaniards in understanding what was happening to them. Their legends had told of these individuals coming to them for as long as they could remember. They would only come when there was a grave illness and many people were in danger of losing their lives. They would always come dressed the same way and would not speak to any of the people, but would go from place to place touching and healing all who they came across. As silently as they appeared on the scene, they would leave in the same way. Each of their visits would be marked by a bright light that would fill the sky and all the land from the outside to the inside and would usually occur on the night after the visit to the people. The Indians came to respect, not worship, these visitors for what they were able to do for them. According to this legend, each of the original locations the people were to locate was marked with a stone inscribed with what they related to that day as funny writing. Only one of the stones remained from all of the original ones and it happened to be located a few miles southeast of the village.

"'After hearing of the Indian's legend, the Spaniards had no reason to doubt it being real after going through what had been. The Spaniards decided to give the individuals a name, a name that reflected a status to these individuals. The name was *Currendero*...'The Healers'.

"'The song legends have it that a similar event has taken place several times over the last three hundred years and the last account of this happening was in 1918 and in the same lands that you are on now.'

"I had doubts in my mind until my great-grandfather, shortly before his death, took me out to a mesa where he showed me a rock with the funny writing. It was like nothing I had ever seen before or since. It just looked like a bunch of little pictures and lines in a rock. What did amaze me was that the rock was impervious to scratches. I tried to make my own mark on it when great-grandfather was not looking, and discovered that no matter how hard I tried that I could not even make a mark on it. Great Grandfather turned and with a motioning to the rock he had just showed me said that here is where no evil can live. He wanted me to remember that there were places in the world like that to let them know his legend story was true so I could pass it on to others when it was time.

"Wind From The East continued with his story.

"'Now the people of the village all decided that they had been given such a great blessing that they should do something that would show the newly discovered visitors that they appreciated what they had done for them. They wanted to erect a great monument to those who had come among them so that they would see it and be pleased with it. They also hoped that by doing such a thing that it would compel them to return and when they did, they would bring ever more blessings with them.

"'What the villagers did was to spend the next thirty years in constructing a huge monument with several carved images of those who had come to their village. They were not satisfied with anything that was small but had pooled all of their resources so that they could make their images as large as their tallest building. All of their time and effort and resources went into building this monument but all that they were doing was for the wrong reasons and it was going in the wrong direction. What was needed by all of them was to go within themselves to better understand what had happened to all of them but instead, they all decided to journey to the outside of themselves and make such a huge edifice that it would be so impressive to those who had come among them that they would not be able to resist themselves in coming back to them again.

"'In the end, the village was left without any food or resources, and for all of their efforts the ones who had come among them did not ever return. They did not ever realize that the gift of life that they were given was given to them so they would be able to live and advance their own spirits. What was not wanted by those who had come among them was what they had done with the additional time that they had been given for the life path they were walking with the Earth Mother.

"'The entire village and all of its inhabitants were forgotten with the passing of many seasons and all of the work that they had performed was for nothing, as you can see by looking over the valley where they once lived. They tired to achieve a greatness of their own by constructing an impressive monument. They did not succeed because the only truth that is in any life path that will last will be the truth that comes from within.

"'That has been the path you have been on, young man. You have been trying to attain your greatness by producing things that are not of the inner self and this has resulted in leaving you very empty on the inside. The attainment of the greatness that you are so desperately seeking lies within yourself only. When you are tired enough to look for it there, you will find all that you have ever dreamed of finding and much more.

"'You are standing at the doorway of a great discovery, young man. I only hope that you will be ready to recognize it for what it is.'

"After finishing his speaking words to me, the old man lowered his head and was looking at the ground that was beneath his feet. He began to sing a very quiet spirit song and it was one that I recognized as being the spirit song of Two Elks and Morning Wind.

"I could tell that our time was over now and rose from the sitting position that I had been in and began to walk back to the opening of the cave. I knew that I had much to think on when a question suddenly came to my mind. I wanted to ask the old man what he meant that I was at the doorway to a great discovery and why he said that he could only hope that I would be ready for it. However, when I turned around to ask him, he was no longer there. The light, too, had gone and there was no trace of either of them having ever been there.

"For the next season, I busied myself with learning about the spirit that was within me and I was very pleased with what I was finding. I also noticed that many of the elders and wise ones of our villages were beginning to seek me out to ask me questions about things that would be brought to them. The old man was right. I had entered the doorway to myself and had found what I was looking for. It was still another season before I met your grandmother but when we met with our eyes, we both recognized each other for who we were and this was the beginning of my greatest quest in the life path that I am now walking with the Earth Mother. It was after we had come together that so many of the mysteries that I had sought to discover had come to me. Together, we traveled a life path that all who came into contact with us enjoyed being close to. We had been two and now we had become one. I was very thankful for the council that Wind From The East had given to me and in the seasons that are yet to come for you, you will both gain much insight to the life path that you are walking, having heard my speaking words to you of this time."

Both Cheeway and I were very surprised at the speaking words that Grandfather was sharing with us. He had not ever shared his past with grandmother before this and it was very interesting for both of us.

"Grandfather," I asked, in a very respectful voice, "why do you choose to share these speaking words with us now?"

"I am sharing these speaking words with the both of you so you will be able to understand why I reacted to the spirit vision of Two Elks and Morning Wind. I am sharing these speaking words to you so that the both of you will understand why you must go through so much in your life paths. I am sharing these speaking words to both of you so that you will understand that there will always be a reason for all that you will experience and go through. I am sharing these speaking words to you so you will understand that all things that happen to each of you will always happen for a reason. The reason they will happen to you will be for the best of reasons…and that is to prepare you for the one you will meet in the time that you have to walk a life path with the Earth Mother.

"I am giving each of you much more than you really are asking for but there is a reason for that as well. At the age both of you are at, the kinds of questions that you are asking are filled with the innocence that is very common for ones of your age. However, I will not always be with you in the life path that you are walking. Because of this, I am planting many seeds within your minds so when you are ready to understand them, you will be able to bring them unto yourselves. Then you will have an adequate level of understanding to remember my speaking words to you from these times. You will each need so much help in all that is ahead of you. The reason that you will need so much help is that there is much preparation that you each will have to do in order to be ready to meet your other half spirit when the time comes."

"Grandfather," Cheeway asked, still sitting on the edges of his feet, "if you had not been ready to meet grandmother and had only passed her by as you would have passed any other person, then what would have happened to all of us?"

"If we had not prepared for each other, then none of this would have been possible."

"Do you mean that none of us would have ever been able to walk a life path with the Earth Mother?"

"What I mean is that the life path that you are currently walking with the Earth Mother would not have been possible. I do not mean that you would not have been able to walk her domain at all. As it is with all of the spirit groups, you would have had to find another of our group to enter into a life path with. But that would have altered many of the lessons that you wished to learn."

"This understanding brings a great responsibility on all of us, Grandfather. Do you mean for us to see it in this way?" I asked, still sitting on the ground that was in front of him.

"Yes, I do. The reasons that I wish to do this are many, but for now, I will only tell you one of the greatest purposes of walking a life path. You are here to learn how to be in control of all things that will happen to each of you and to learn to take the full responsibility for all that will happen by your actions.

"It is always easier to see the path that gives the most comfort but this is the path that those who will not accomplish any spiritual advancement take. Both of you will advance not only your own spirits but those of our entire group by succeeding in all of the quests that will be set before each of you. In order to do this, you must take the path that will lead you to more learning and under-standing of yourselves.

"Just as it was for me, so shall it be for the both of you. What you will be able to accomplish as individuals will always be tied to each other. When the time comes and you will meet your other half spirit, that is when the most ben-eficial portions of your work will begin."

"Grandfather," I said, "you also mentioned that you would tell us of some of the warning signs that would be seen by us. You remember…the ones that you said would come to us before the great catastrophe would come over all of the Earth Mother's domain."

"Yes, I remember that. Would you like me to go into that now?"

Both Cheeway and I were shaking our heads in an up and down manner. We knew that Grandfather would have no doubt in his mind that we were not only willing to listen to the speaking words he would share with us on this subject, but we were very anxious to hear about them as well.

CHAPTER 11

❁

The Reminding of Why Spirits Touch

"For as long as our people's collective memory that is contained in all of our song legends and rock paintings, there have been these signs that would come to those who would have the eyes to see them with.

"It is not anything that is new, just as it is not anything that is new about meeting your other half spirit in the life path that you are walking. However, it is very rare that this knowledge is recognized because it requires some rather uncomfortable work in order to achieve it.

"Our people's song legends tell us of a time that this had happened before. These same kinds of events that happened then will happen once again. It was a time when our people that had been walking their life path with the Earth Mother had many blessings. There were no illnesses and suffering and the length of each life path was given ten fold from what we have in the days we are in now.

"Because of all of the misuse of the gifts that the Earth Mother had given to us, our people had become very oriented to the needs of the body and had all but forgotten about their spirits that were within themselves.

"Because the spirit had been forgotten, there were many important laws that are very basic to the Earth Mother's that were not being followed. One of these laws that were forgotten was the one that told all of our people that a union between any two people should not be taken lightly. That when two people come together in a union, there were many responsibilities that would have to be taken on.

"Originally, our people would always wait until many seasons passed over the life path they were walking before they would even make an attempt of finding their mate. The reason for this was given to all of us as one of giving ourselves sufficient time to prepare ourselves for the one that we would share our life path with.

"Our people knew that if any were to attempt to be joined before our preparations were complete, that the chance of joining to the one that was not right for the other was greatly increased. Any union that was attempted in this way would not be fair to either of them, nor would it be fair to the one that they were truly right for.

"In the beginning, our people lived with this basic rule of the Earth Mother and all things went very well. All would give their individual life path sufficient time so that they would be able to experience enough and work through enough to build and understand the true side of themselves.

"All of their eyes and hearts were being opened and in the correct way. You see when you are young and inexperienced, you have a tendency to run toward someone in hopes of escaping from those things that we perceive as our problems in life. We will do most anything that will keep us from having to work through our own problems as they are seen by the younger side of the person. However, as we become older and have learned to work through more of these events that have happened to us, we gain an understanding of ourselves and come to realize that there will not ever be a situation that can happen to us that cannot be solved. That solution lies within ourselves.

"It is in this way that our eyes and hearts are opened up. It is in this way that this process takes place as it was designed to take place. When we have reached this place in our spiritual development, we understand so much more about ourselves. We are able to better present ourselves to the one who has been preparing for us.

"However, as the seasons of the Earth Mother passed, it was becoming less and less of a practice among our people to wait for this process to develop them. When this process was developed with them, the children that would come to them would always be from their own spiritual group and there was not ever any strangeness among any of the members of their family. Now, in many seasons later, many of our people were not following the procedures that the Earth Mother had set before them to follow and were creating unions long before they were ready.

"One thing that both of you must remember is that when the body is not knowledgeable enough of the spirit that lives with in, there will not be any room for love. The only emotion that will be available will be the fascination of the newness of another that is in your life. The feeling has a very short life path to walk with you and you will find that one morning when you wake up, you will look at the other and wonder who they really are.

"The reason for this is there was not sufficient time that went into preparing yourself. You have ended up with one who was meant for another. This will cause many problems. One that comes to mind is that both of these people will always feel as though they have a part of their own life that is missing.

"When this happens, one of two things will occur. Either the two people will stay together but not from any love that they may have for each other but out of guilt, or they will leave each other.

"One of the sad events that happens in this type of misperception of what the Earth Mother had set before them to do is that they will often have offspring during the course of their union. Within the normal set of instructions that the Earth Mother had given to our people in those days, it was set into the minds of all who would come to her to walk a life path that when they would follow the procedure that she had set for them, all of the offspring that would come to them would be only those from their own spirit group. This would create a comfortable feeling of familiarity among the entire family and they would all benefit by being able to grow together.

"However, because her guidelines were not being followed, there were many offspring who were coming to these people who had joined in a union from different spiritual groups. One of the spiritual groups would be from the father and one would be from the mother. This created many problems because only one of the parents would feel comfortable with the child that had come to them. In a short time, the other parent would begin to feel left out and eventually leave to find another home.

"When this happens, all who are concerned will be made to suffer and this was not the original intent of what the Earth Mother had in mind for our people who would come to her. She wanted all that would walk a life path with her to be able to find their other half spirit when they would be available. If they were not available in the life path they were walking with her, then the lessons that were to be learned from her were supposed to be learned in a singular way. This is the rationale of the spirit. However, the rationale of the body is different. The body only recognizes that it has certain desires that it needs to satisfy.

Whatever it needs to satisfy them, it will do. This was another sign of the beginning period before the last great catastrophe transpired.

"From the result of what these children would see in their early years, it was carrying over to the next generation and the next and so on until the formula that the Earth Mother had originally set for them was forgotten by the majority. This resulted in many spirits coming to walk a life path with the Earth Mother who did not having an anchoring system that would show them what the correct spiritual values were. As a result of this, the majority of these spirits were listening only to the demands of the body, which is temporary at best. When a temporary being tries to understand the balance of the life path they are walking, it does not make any sense to them. In order to understand the value lessons that are to be gained while walking a life path, one must be able to comprehend more than the temporary existence. The only direction that the mind of the body can conceive of are those things that are as temporary as itself.

"When one is prepared and their spirit touches the one they were intended for, then all of the clarity that is needed by them is given. Once this point is reached, all of those things they have learned are understood. They will see how well they each have prepared themselves for each other. When this is not done, as was the case in those days of old, there were just a great number of spirits walking a life path that had no idea of any direction that they should follow. All of the things that will happen to them will not be perceived as necessary for their preparation and spiritual growth. Instead, they will only be seen as problems and they will try to avoid them with all of the energies at their disposal.

"Although there were still a few who remembered the ways of the old ones and they tried to teach these values to the others, it was to no avail. By this time, all of our people were so confused that they could only perceive their life path as a series of problems. All of their efforts were spent in trying to run away from them. This resulted in each one of them looking out only for themselves.

"This made the Earth Mother and the spirits of the land very angry and sad at the same time. Instead of stopping all of the spirits from visiting her domain and learning the lessons that were very necessary for their spiritual advancement, they decided to call together the great council of seven. It was from this great council that a decision was made.

"It was decided that all of the life paths should be substantially reduced in the amount of time that they would be able to walk with the Earth Mother and there would no longer be a pain and suffering freedom which all of the spirits had enjoyed. It was also decided that all of the memories that had been retained by all of the spirits walking a life path with the Earth Mother would be taken away and would only come back after a great deal of work on the path that leads to within where the spirit resides.

"These were some of the import signs that had come among our people before the last great catastrophe. These will be the same signs that will come before the next one. From what I have told the both of you, you will be able to see when this time is near because all that had happened before will happen once again."

PART IV

❀

PATH TO THE SPIRIT

CHAPTER 12

❀

Three Stages to Preparation

Grandfather looked at the both of us as we sat there with our mouths hanging open. We could tell that he was looking deep within each of us for some clues that we had both understood what it was that he was saying.

"Do you have any questions regarding the speaking words that I have shared with the both of you?" Grandfather asked Cheeway and myself, as he continued to stare into each of us with his eyes.

"Yes, Grandfather," I said, still sitting on the same piece of ground that I had been on when he began. "You tell both of us that we each have our other half spirit walking a life path just like the both of us are doing. You have also told us that if we are not prepared for the other one, then we will pass each other by just as we would pass another stranger or casual acquaintance."

"Yes, this is the truth in what I have shared with both of you," Grandfather said, looking more attentively at me now.

"Why do you ask this question?"

"Well, Grandfather," I said, sitting more erect now. "If we pass our other half spirit by because we were not prepared to meet them and we have a need or a desire to join with another, will we become like our people were those many generations ago?"

"I am afraid that you will," Grandfather said, as he bent his head down and toward the ground he was sitting on. "I can only hope for both of your sakes that you will not let such an opportunity pass you by. I can tell you both, that what I have experienced by being able to walk my life path with your grandmother, that there is nothing else like it in the entire domain of the Earth

Mother. You will find that your entire life will change and it will change for the better. All that had been unclear to both of you will become as clear as the waters of the lake of tears on our lands of the mesa.

"You must both remember that when you will make your decision to create a union with another, it is your spirits that will determine the level of happiness that you will be able to find."

Grandfather was looking at Cheeway and I. We knew that he could see that we were not very clear on what he had just shared with us.

"The teachings of our people tell us that the number three is very special to all things that affect our life path. This also applies to the three stages of awareness that we must all pass through in order to have a successful life path.

"The first of these stages is the body's domain. It is in this stage where all of the terrible things will always seem to happen to you. Or at least, this is how it will be perceived by one who is in this stage of their life path. In this stage, everything that happens seems to happen only to you. In your own mind, nothing so bad has or could ever have happened to anyone else.

"From the first stage, you will find the majority of people will think of themselves in terms that they are the center of all things. It is from here that the world seems to revolve around them. This becomes apparent from all that they will do or say. It is also a place where they will not see anyone else's pain or suffering. They will only see theirs and will spend their time wondering why others cannot see how they are suffering.

"This stage of the life path is usually attributed to small children, but as you pass more and more seasons, you will see that there are many older ones who also fall into this category. Those who will choose this life path cannot see any further than their own suffering. The fact that they are the ones who are responsible for creating and staying in it is not seen by them. A union that is made in this stage will ultimately lead to disaster because each individual who joins to another in this place of development will only bring more suffering and sadness into the relationship. Neither one of them is ready to join with another. Once the newness of the body walks away for them, they will find themselves two very unhappy spirits and they will see that they do not know the other one they have joined themselves to.

"The second stage of the life path is the one where the spirit is the most prominent player. In this stage, the spirit has been allowed to come into the realm of the body but only for very brief periods of time. Because it has been seen on rare occasions, the person believes that this is the end result of what their life should be. They use those brief encounters with their own spirit as what all life should be like. This also results, from those who will stay in this stage of development, in their forcing their way onto others they will come into contact with. Those who reside in this stage will not allow others who are close to them have any freedom of their own. They will not be tolerant of any other way of life that is different from the one they feel they have discovered from their one brief encounter with their own spirit.

"The spirit has not been able to communicate to them that what they have experienced is only a beginning because they have chosen to close off the channel that it wants to give to them. Because these people have only seen bits and pieces of their own spirit as it would come to them, they are not as sure of its ability of coming back to them. Because of this, they are doubtful of its return. They hold onto the small glimpse of this spiritual reality in a very insecure way.

"This doubt causes them to tell rather than to share the ways that lead to understanding the balance of the life path. Their telling comes in the way that they will sculpture their speaking words to most anyone who will listen to them. You can see them as they stand before many people and speak of the one or two experiences that they have had.

"These few encounters with the emergence of their spirit to themselves becomes their only meaningful experience. Because of this, they look only on this for all of the things that they will address to others. They have stopped their spiritual advancement because instead of anticipating the future with all of its possibilities and lessons that are to be learned, they only address their past and attempt to explain away all things that happen to them in this day by their old experiences. At no time, do the ones who are in this second stage of development look ahead of them. Their world is their past and will continue to stay there unless they work through this and into the third stage of the life path.

"Any union made in this second stage of the life path will partially succeed but its success will not be from the position of the body's terms. It will be from the memory of a spiritual encounter that has happened to these two people many seasons ago. Their union will live as a memory does. There will be nothing that will come to either of them as new life. They will stay with each other only to hold onto those things that they were not ever sure of before they joined. However, if only one of these two goes further, and into the third stage of the life path, there will be the other who will stay behind because of insecurity or from the fear of change...and then their union will be doomed to failure.

"You see, in this second stage of the life path, a union to another is made on a gamble. That gamble is that either both of the of the two people will stay where they are in this second stage together, or they must both jointly enter into the third stage of the life path. If only one of them will do this, and the other is left behind, it becomes a great possibility that the one left behind will fall back into the first stage of the life path and they will have no balance of understanding between them.

"The possibility of entering the third stage of the life path with another is very rare because of the changes that will be encountered in order to cross through its doors. The path is very difficult for just one to enter, so you can get an idea of how difficult it could become for two to enter together.

"This doorway is very strong. I have seen many others who try to enter through it literally bounce off of it and fall on the ground where they were walking. However, when I see only one who will make it through this door, the rewards in their spiritual growth become so great that everything else seems very small.

"The third stage of the life path is the one that is the most desirable for all of us who walk a life path with the Earth Mother. It is here that we will find our most important balances that will allow us to understand those things that we have come here to learn.

"This is the stage where all that we have done, in the many seasons that we have walked through, will come to us with such clarity and purpose that we cannot help but see the trueness of design by the Great Spirit, the Earth Mother, and the spirits of the land.

"In this stage, all things will be shown to us. It will become clear that all we have gone through and experienced had been for a specific reason. That reason was a design that will allow us to be ready to meet our other half spirit.

"Now, when you have been patient with the ways of our people and the balance of understanding of the life path you are on, you are prepared to meet your other half spirit. When this meeting occurs, you will not need any time to know that this is the one who has been equally prepared, just as you have. You will know within a matter of a few minutes that this other person is a very intricate part of your destiny and the growth will begin immediately."

Grandfather paused with his speaking words for a few moments and looked at Cheeway and myself with another one of his intense looks. He showed us both a large smile that sat very well on his face and then he continued.

"You will both continue to have shared experiences in the life path you are walking. What I mean is, you will see the entire sequence of events that have lead up to both of you being prepared to meet.

"When this time comes, you will be standing in a sun filled day and there will be a tree that you will become very close to. For reasons that are not known to me at this time, I see both of you, but in separate times and places look up from whatever it is that you will be doing and see a woman walking toward you. For both of you, the experience will be very much the same. These two women will be wearing a dark blue material with white filled in circles located inside of the material.

"From the time that you will first see her, there will be a sense of something very familiar about her. You will continue to look at her trying to figure out what it is that you are seeing that seems so familiar to you. She will be walking to you because this is how it happens. When she comes to you at last, you will both sit in a place that is very comfortable and you will begin talking about things that are not very important to either of you.

"This conversation is being performed because it will be both of your ways to conceal the fact that you are looking into the other's spirit. Both of you will come to the other with completely equal abilities and this is very necessary. If either of you will come to your other half spirit with anything less, then the other one would not be able to communicate with you and that would be a terrible loss. However, what I see for the both of you is that this will not happen because this initial encounter will not fail.

"As you continue your conversations, each of you travel inside the other's spirit. You will be taken to a place that is not familiar to either of you, but it will be for such a short time that it will be hardly noticed. This will be the time when your spirits will touch and the beginning of your life with your completeness will have begun.

"From that point on, both of you will begin to change. The change that will come to you will not be fought but will be welcomed because of the love, the peace, and the security that you will feel for the other. What begins on this day that I see for both of you is the beginning of your reward. This is the return for all that you all will have gone through and you will see the purpose to all living things that are. You will discover that all you thought you knew and understood was only a part because of what the other one will bring to you. It will make you aware of so much more that many of the lessons of the past will uncover themselves to you in all of their completeness. This completeness that will come to you will not be possible with the other's coming. I see success for both of you. You will be continually amazed at all of the sharing of life and love that will transpire between you."

"Grandfather," I asked, "can you tell us when this time will come?"

"This I cannot do because it has not been decided yet. I can only tell both of you that this time will come to you and when it does, it will make all that you have done and experienced before seem like only half of what it once did."

PART V

※

WHEN THE SPIRIT SEES

CHAPTER 13

❀

Speaking Words From Two Bears

We had returned from the mesa in Grandfather's truck and all of the speaking words that he had shared with Cheeway and myself was causing both of us to do great amounts of thinking within ourselves.

Grandfather had dropped both of us at Cheeway's parents' house and had driven to another village where he told us that he had pressing business with some of the village elders. We knew very well that to question him on things that he was not willing to discuss would get us nothing but very tired. We got out of the truck and walked to the back of Cheeway's parents' house where there was a large open area where we would usually go to play.

This day, neither Cheeway nor myself felt like playing. We decided to just spend our time on this land thinking of all of the speaking words that Grandfather had shared with us.

"Cheeway," I said, picking up one of the smaller stones that was on this land and throwing it far into the distance, "what do you think of the speaking words that Grandfather has shared with us."

"I do not know," Cheeway said, mirroring my throwing stones out to the open lands that were before us. "I only know that whatever Grandfather shares with is for a reason. Do you remember what he told us when he said that much of what he was going to share with us would not be understood by us at this time? Well, I think that we are going to have to wait for a long time before much of this makes more sense to either of us."

"I believe that you are right, Cheeway. I only wish that more understanding was available to us. Then we would be able to ask Grandfather questions about pieces that we did not understand. Instead, if we were to ask him questions now, I believe that we would spend more time on this one subject than he has time left to him."

"I agree," Cheeway said. "Maybe we will get a flash of insight into these things and be able to question him on things that would even surprise him. Wouldn't that be fun?"

"It would be fun, Cheeway, but I do not believe that we will be able to enjoy that, at least not for the seasons that we have seen so far."

I could see that Cheeway was shaking his head in an up and down manner to show me that he was agreeing with the speaking words that we had shared. With this out of the way, we continued throwing stones into the open lands that were before us. Soon, we were lost in our world of play.

"Hello!" came a voice from behind us.

Both Cheeway and I turned to see who had been able to sneak up on us so successfully. When we turned our vision to the direction where the sound had come from, we were relieved to see that it was Two Bears and he was already sitting on the ground that was behind us.

"You both must have great thoughts on your minds to allow such an old man like me to walk up behind you and even sit down before you noticed. What is going through your minds that you would wish to share with me?"

We could see that the look that was on the face of Two Bears was a very kind and understanding one. He and Grandfather had been together since they were born. All things that Grandfather understood were also understood by Two Bears.

I looked over in the direction of where Cheeway was standing and could see that he also wanted to tell Two Bears of all the speaking words that Grandfather had shared with us. We both knew that since Two Bears was as knowledgeable as Grandfather, then perhaps he would be able to shed more understanding into the speaking words that Grandfather had shared with us on the mesa earlier that day.

"Two Bears," I said facing him, "We would like to share some of the speaking words that Grandfather has shared with us. The reason that we want to share them with you is to ask you if you could add your clarity of thought to them.

"Most of the speaking words that Grandfather has shared with us this day do not make much sense to us," Cheeway said, looking rather helpless as he was standing on the opposite side of where Two Bears was sitting.

"Well, little ones, it would seem to me that the best place for you both to begin would be at the beginning. Now, why don't you both have a seat on this land with me and I will listen to all that you wish to share. Perhaps after I hear what it is that you wish to tell me, then I might be able to add a little more to it."

Cheeway looked at me with a look on his face that was asking me if I thought it would be alright to do this. I nodded my head to him in an up and down manner so he would be able to see that I thought it would be. Seeing my approval, all three of us sat on this land that was behind the house.

For the next hour or so, we told Two Bears of all the speaking words that Grandfather had shared with us. We could see from the look that he placed on his face that he was very surprised with some of the things that he had chosen to share with us.

"Little Ones," Two Bears said, looking at both of us, "I am sure that your Grandfather had his reasons for telling you of these things. If you would, I would also enjoy hearing why he would choose to tell you, who are of so few seasons, things that are for a more advanced mind."

"Grandfather had told us that his seasons that are left to him are very few now. If he did not tell us of these things now, then there might not be time for us to hear them from him. He also told us that all of the things that he was sharing with both of us would become necessary for each of us in order to succeed on our life path."

Two Bears looked at both of us and could see that there was a very kind and understanding look that had come into his eyes. We both knew that what we were seeing in him was a love that he held for all things that were from the Earth Mother. These things that Grandfather had shared with the both of us coupled with the knowledge that Grandfather did not have much longer to walk a life path made Two Bears very willing to share with us.

Cheeway and I looked at each other and both understood that we were going to acquire more speaking words from Two Bears. They, too, would be the kind that would make sense to us, as we would pass through more seasons in our life path. We could tell that Two Bears was not going to attempt to clarify the speaking words that Grandfather had shared with us, instead, he was going to add to them. So Cheeway and I just sat back against one of the rocks that was on our lands and prepared ourselves to listen to what Two Bears would add to our collective memory.

"When the spirit sees, there will be no mistaking it for either of you. This is a time when you will realize that you have attained a level of understanding that has not been reached by many. Now, when two spirits touch…this is a blessing that is among the greatest throughout all of the domain that is the Earth Mother's and it, too, is a rare thing for any to find."

Two Bears lifted his head toward the clear blue sky that was over our lands. We could tell that he was silently asking the spirits of the land to guide his speaking words to the both of us because they were so important. Seeing this, we both felt a great presence among the three of us and feeling this presence, Two Bears returned his head to where we were sitting.

Looking at us and smiling, he continued with his speaking words.

CHAPTER 14

The Tree of Life Song Legend

"You both know of our song legends of the tree of life and how each leaf that is on it represents a spirit who is walking a life path with the Earth Mother?"

We both shook our heads in an up and down manner to tell Two Bears that we knew of this song legend.

"There are many things about the leaves that must be kept in mind as I continue with my speaking words to the both of you. Each leaf is a symbolic reminder that there is an accompanying spirit walking a life path with us. You must see the full cycle of the development of these leaves as they grow and eventually fall off from the branch that they are on in order to understand that which I am willing to share with you.

"As each leaf will develop on one of the branches of the tree of life, some will continue on as they should be and develop into a full leaf. However, you will encounter others who will be walking a life path with you, that will not develop into a full leaf on the tree of life and will only hold their position on their branch returning nothing for what they are taking.

"Those leaves who will develop into what they should be will take the things from the tree of life that will give them the life force they require, and in return, they will give their breathing air to all who will need it. Now, those leaves that do not develop but remain as a bud, they will only take the life force from the tree of life but since they will not develop into that which they were designed to become, they will not complete their useful purpose. They will only take up the space where another leaf could be placed.

"So we know that from all of the spirits who will ever come to walk a life path with the Earth Mother that not all of them will know the meaning of achieving their true potential. Not all will understand the values that are hidden in the life path that they are walking. Not only will their life path become unmeaningful, but they will also take up the space where another could have been placed.

"We look at all of these unfortunate spirits and shake our heads sadly. They will not ever know the joys their life path could have brought them through understanding the meaning of the many lessons they set before themselves. They will not advance their spirit. However, we do not say anything to them because we realize that this is not our place to tell them. We have been taught that it is enough for us to recognize that these spirits are the ones that we must stay away from. If we try to change them, they will only bring us down to their level over time. Our teachings tell us that it is a mistake to try to help them and think our strength will be enough to keep us and them above their level. If we attempt to do this, we will soon find ourselves living in their level. Our efforts of raising them to ours do not work.

"Now, both of you understand that not all the spirits who will attempt to walk a life path with the Earth Mother will bring benefit to anyone. I will remind you both that their numbers are greater than the ones who will attempt to understand themselves. If you could see the tree of life, you would understand my speaking words better. To look at it is to see its branches covered with many buds but there are very few open leaves on it.

"With those leaves that remain in their useful form, there will be only a very small portion of them who will be able to understand the full effect of the life path they have set before them. It is from this level of understanding that they will know what it is that they will have to perform in order to have a successful life path.

"As you can see, the numbers have already become much smaller from those that had started out as a bud on the tree of life. Those very few, who will understand the balance of the life path, will understand that in time, they will be able to accomplish all that they had set out to perform. They will feel their spirits grow within them.

"Once they have reached that point, they will be given a choice. That choice will come to them with the dream spirit. It will ask them if they wish to return to the waiting place across the great spirit waters.

"When this choice is given to them, they will see all things that they have encountered and will understand them. They will be shown the waiting place and all of the beauty that it holds for them. They will also be shown that all who have gone before them are there and they will see the smiles on their faces that come from being in a place that is in full balance with the Great Spirit. They will feel the peace and joy that is there and will be offered their place in it.

"The other choice that will be given to them will be the one where they will be allowed to continue walking their life path with the Earth Mother for the remainder of the time that had been originally set aside for them. They will understand that if they choose to come back to the Earth Mother for this time that all of the quests that will be placed before them will not only benefit them, but will also advance the entire spirit family that they are a part of. The blessings that will be bestowed upon them will be great.

"From all of those who will be given this opportunity, only a few of them will be blessed with being able to be with their other half spirit, who is walking a life path in the same time that they are.

"Now, we have really reduced the total numbers of those spirits that we have been talking about. In all, if you will see one thousand spirits walking a life path before you, there will only be twelve who will be given this opportunity. Those who will be given this opportunity of meeting and being with their other half spirit will find that if they choose to remain with the Earth Mother for what remains of their time here, and in order to be with their other half spirit, all the things that they will be able to accomplish together will be of such great and lasting value to so many that it will become almost impossible for them to comprehend.

"All of those things that will result from their union in their life path together will last as long as the spirit of life will continue in the tree of life. Because of their accomplishments, the tree of life will be given another branch on which other leaves may be placed.

"These speaking words that I have chosen to share with the both of you are another way of telling you those things that Grandfather has told you. We are trying to tell the both of you that each of you will have the opportunity of becoming one of those twelve in one thousand, if you choose to accept that which has been set before you. We realize that much of what we will share with you will not be fully understood by either of you. But we also realize that you will be able to recall all of these speaking words when the time will come that you will have need of them. You see in the many seasons that Grandfather and I have spent with the Earth Mother, we have learned how to speak to the spirit that lives within each of us. All things that the spirit will hear will not be forgotten. This is why we are able to say to both of you that you will be able to recall those things that we have shared with you in your younger seasons. When we speak to both of you on these things, it is your spirits that we are speaking to and not just the ears that are located on the outside."

Two Bears had finished his speaking words to both Cheeway and myself and was now looking at the few slow moving clouds that were blessing our lands. While Two Bears was looking at the clouds that were being led by the wind spirit, I was looking at him and for the first time since I had known him, I could see him in a much different way.

The Two Bears that I had known had become a very tall and strong spirit. Because of the wisdom that he had shared with Cheeway and myself on this day, I knew that some of the things that Grandfather had shared with us were beginning to make some sense. One of these things was that there would not ever be a day that I would not have to work at attaining a higher level of understanding of myself. I knew on this day that one of the purposes of walking a life path with the Earth Mother was not to sit by and wait for things to come to me, but it would be up to me to find those things that I was seeking for myself. I realized that this continual process of learning was going to be with me for all of the time that I would spend in the domain of the Earth Mother. The benefit from this would be that one day I would possess the wisdom and strength that I had seen in Grandfather and Two Bears.

"Two Bears," I asked, still sitting in the same position that we had all started out in, "will there ever be a time when we do not learn from the life path we are on?"

Two Bears slowly lowered his head from its position towards the sky and to one that was looking at both of us and said, "Yes, there will be a time when you may stop the continual learning. However, you must understand that when this happens, all of the spiritual advancement that both of you are looking for will also come to a complete stop."

"So you mean that if we are to achieve those things that we intend to accomplish, we will not ever be able to take a short rest from this?" came the speaking words from Cheeway.

"This is exactly what I mean, Cheeway. You must keep in your mind that you are not here to rest. That will come later for all of us. We are here with the Earth Mother to learn all that she will be able to teach us. It will be from this learning that we will be able to advance our spirits sufficiently to become one with the Great Spirit once again."

CHAPTER 15

❀

The Power Steps

Two Bears paused for a moment. He was looking into both of us as we were sitting in front of him on our lands. And as he was looking into each of us in turn, we could feel his eyes searching for something within us but we did not know what it was that he was looking for.

Just as suddenly as he began his looking, he continued his speaking words to us.

"Do both of you understand what it is to place a picture of what it is that you want in your minds so that it will come to be?"

Cheeway and I were both looking at Two Bears in complete wonder. While we were understanding the speaking words he was sharing with us, we did not grasp their implied meaning and Two Bears recognized this in both of us.

"When you will look at the many teachings of our people, there will be many things that you will find making more sense to you. This will be from the additional seasons that both of you will have passed through and you will have acquired much more experience that you will be able to draw on. This will give you a higher level of understanding for those things that will come to you in the way of lessons.

"This will be another of those instances when you may not completely understand these speaking words that I am sharing with you. In time, and when you will have a need for them, they will come back to you filled with wisdom and direction."

"Is this because you are speaking to our spirits once again, Two Bears?" Cheeway asked, as he adjusted his sitting position once again.

"Yes, Cheeway. It is because I am speaking to both your body and your spirit that will allow you to go back and recall these speaking words when the time is right."

We both looked at Two Bears and were shaking our heads in an up and down manner that would tell him that we not only understood, but that we were in agreement with this process that he was employing with each of us.

"Our teachings are very old and so much of what they have to offer us is filled with great wisdom. However, as you will find in so much of the life path the both of you will walk, there will not be many who you will come across that will ever be ready to embrace these truths because of the truths they believe they know.

"As with all things that will follow each of you in the life path you are on, there will be times when the body will become the driving force in all of us. When we listen to the truths that are resting in our people's teachings, we can feel very guilty when these teachings show us that we have gotten off the path that leads us to the understanding of the balance of the life path. Since this will not be seen as a good feeling when it is true, there will be a great temptation to turn away from it. You see, the body does not like confrontation nor does it like to be reminded that it is just a temporary traveling vessel. When anything comes to it that reminds it of its place, it will do all that is within its power to tell the spirit within that this knowledge is not worth while and to ignore it.

"The teachings that I share with you are ones that will allow you to create a picture in your minds of what it is that you will wish for. It will be a technique that has long been employed by our people and its rate of success, if the proper steps are followed, is extraordinarily high.

"In order to succeed in whatever it is that you wish to accomplish, there must be the dream or picture of what it is that you wish to attain. When this has been accomplished, then it is simply a matter of going in the right direction and holding onto that picture of what you wish to have in your life path.

"All who enter a life path with the Earth Mother have many abilities of doing all that is necessary to attain all that they will need. However, it requires belief and the strength of spirit in order to hold onto this picture dream before it can come into being.

"There will be many things that you will recognize as being necessary to accomplish in order to succeed in the quest that you have put yourselves on. Once you accept this, then the teachings that I am about to share with you will come into play.

"At first, you will see what it is that you wish to accomplish. This will come to you as a completed event. You must be able to see and feel what it will be like to have and hold this event. The beginning is to walk and sleep with this picture in your minds until it becomes a reality to you. That is, when you each have held this picture and felt the successful accomplishment, then it will begin to take on its own life form within you.

"When it begins to take on a life form within you, your spirit will show you all of the events that must happen before you can actually get there. As these stepping stones of events that must happen first begin to take place, you will see the direction of the path you must travel in order to attain your quest. Once you see this, you must travel this path while not ever letting go of the picture that has begun to have its life form within you.

"All of those short stepping stones of events that must take place while you are traveling to your goal will serve as short achievements and as you achieve each one of them, they will serve you well. This is also very necessary, because by achieving these short stepping stones, they will show you that you are traveling the correct path. They will fill you with more and more strength. This strength will carry you to the next one and then the next one until you finally arrive at the final stage of the goal you have given to yourself.

"With each short stepping stone accomplished, you will find that the life form of your desired goal will take on more of a life. You will be able to draw on its strength to assist you in going forward until you finally arrive at where you had wished to be.

"Now, I must also tell the both of you that there is a warning that I am compelled to tell you about as well. This will be the same truth as it was for our ancestors, as it will become for the both of you.

"Once you begin this journey process, you will not ever be able to return to the way that you once were. This is not to scare either of you. It is only meant to inform both of you of what lies ahead.

"Look at it in this way. When you are very young ones as you are now and you pass through each season of your life path, there is not any way for either of you to go back to the place you were when you were much younger. This is the same as with the spiritual journey that I have just shared with you. When you have experienced the first of your spiritual successes, then all that you had been before will not ever be again. You will find that there will be no thing that will be denied to you once you allow your spirit to guide you through your life path. Then it will be the body that will take a back seat to the spirit and great truths will be unveiled to both of you.

"From these truths will come the understanding that seems to be so far away from both of you at this time. Each successful journey using this spiritual technique will mature your spirit more and you will feel yourself advancing swiftly in the life path that you are walking with the Earth Mother.

"Do either of you have any questions about this lesson before I go on to the next one?"

Cheeway and I were sitting on the ground of our lands with both eyes and mouths wide open. Even if we had wanted to nod our heads in an up and down manner we could both feel that the weight of Two Bears speaking words to both of us were so heavy that we would not have been able to. So, we just continued to sit and stare and listen to the speaking words that Two Bears was sharing with both of us.

I did not think that there was this much wisdom in the whole of the Earth Mother's domain as what Grandfather and Two Bears had shared with us, and now Two Bears was going to share more.

CHAPTER 16

❀

Spirit of the Lessons Offered

"I realize that this is very much for the both of you to go through. However, this is necessary because both of you will need this information and our time that is left with the Earth Mother is limited.

"Normally, information such as this would not be passed to any so young as the both of you. However, from what Grandfather has told me of the both of you, all of the information that we are able to give to you from our people's teachings will be of great value to what you must do. There will come a time when both of you will be required to reach from deep within yourselves and pull this information out so that it may see the light of the Great Spirit. When it does, it will grow within many others who you will come into contact with.

"Both of you will come across many opportunities to advance your spirits. You must always remember that they are confronting you to teach you valuable lessons. You should not mistake them, as being something that has been set before you to make you want to run away from them.

"For those who try to hide or run away from their lessons, their passing from this life path with the Earth Mother will go as the dry leaves in the wind. Their deeds will go unnoticed and their memory will only be carried by their group of family that remembers them. Their contribution to others that will walk a life path with the Earth Mother will not be felt.

"However, for all those who you will both meet who do not run away or try to hide from their lessons, their contribution to the others will be great. Many will continue to speak of them long after they have crossed the great spirit waters to the waiting place. Those who work their way through their lessons will attain a great level of understanding. They will be aware of all of the talents that have been given to them by the Great Spirit. They will know what they must do in the time that has been given to them. Stay close to these people and listen to all of the words that they will be willing to share with you. From their speaking words, you will both find many great truths and from these truths, you will be able to increase your own level of understanding in the life path you are walking."

"Two Bears," I asked, still sitting next to Cheeway, "will only certain life paths be designed to greatness?"

"All life paths are designed to greatness, little one," Two Bears said, as he placed a very gentle smile on his face.

"But from the speaking words that we have shared with Grandfather and you, both Cheeway and I are led to believe that our life paths are designed to be great. Is this not so?"

"Yes, little one, this is so. Why do you ask me such a question?"

"It is because of what you have just told us, Two Bears," I said, adjusting myself on the land as I was taking the time to properly address my question. "If our life paths are designed to be great and accomplish many things for others to learn from, then how are we any different than the others who will cross our life path that we are to help?"

"This difference has a presumed beginning. This is what Grandfather and I see as being accomplished by the both of you. You will only be successful if you will follow our teachings.

"There are three things that you both have that many others who are walking a life path do not have. First, you have Grandfather and I who are teaching you many important lessons from the past and present teachings of our people on the mesa. Second, because of these teachings, you both will be better equipped to travel within yourselves and attain the level of understanding that is necessary for you to discover not only the quest that you have each set before yourselves, but also to discover the talents that have been given to you both by the Great Spirit. Thirdly, when you have discovered what you must do with these talents that have been given to you, you will find that you carry many more talents than those others because you have come to know them.

"These three things that I speak to both of you about will determine the level of success that you and others like you will attain. Without all three of them being fully developed, none will be able to succeed fully.

"This is why it is so important for you to learn to use the word lesson in all that will come before you. If you will learn 'lesson' well, then it will make much more sense for you to learn to work through things instead of trying to run away or hide from them.

"Lesson will give you the ability of being in control of any situation that may come your way. If you are in control of things, then they cannot control you."

Once again, Two Bears turned his attention to some of the small white clouds that were crossing our lands on the mesa. We could see that he was going deep within himself to find more speaking words to share with Cheeway and myself. As we continued to look at him, we could see him as a very old man but also as being very young and filled with the life of one who has discovered many secrets. There were times during the sharing of speaking words that both Cheeway and I saw a kind of inner laughing come over his face. It was one that we both recognized as a joy of knowing many truths that were within the domain of the Earth Mother. This was why we considered his speaking words with the same weight that we accepted Grandfather's.

In a rather quick motion, Two Bears turned his attention from the rolling clouds above us to the position where we were sitting and continued with his speaking words.

"There is a very simple and dear secret that I wish to share with the both of you."

When Cheeway and I heard these speaking words come out of Two Bears, we both sat up immediately in order to listen to all that he was going to share with us.

"We are walking this life path with the Earth Mother encased in a traveling shell which holds our spirits. This shell has been loaned to us by the Earth Mother herself and it has been created with the same great magic that she has created all of her children with. The secret that I wish to share with you is this.

"As you both will pass through more and more seasons in the life path that you are on, you will take on all of the attributes of a tree. All trees begin from a seed in the Earth Mother and in the end, they will return to her once again. However, as each of these trees grow, they will send their roots throughout all of the lands that have been made available to them to receive the food and water to continue its life. As its life continues, it will grow into a great communicator between the Earth Mother, the spirits of the land and the Earth Mother's children.

"Look at the trees that you will pass very closely. You will see that some of them look very strong and straight. Others look like they are near their death even before they are very old. Some will be crooked and bent and will have very few leaves on them. This is because each of these trees will grow only to the level of what they have been given and how they have been treated.

"This is the same for those others who will cross your life path in the many seasons yet to come for the both of you. Those who have learned to nurture themselves with thoughts that are good and pure will mature into very tall and straight people and they will be blessed with very good health and a mind that allows its spirit to share the life path with it."

Two Bears looked at the both of us in silence and we could tell that there were many thoughts that were running through his mind as he was doing this.

"Two Bears," I asked, still sitting in the same position that I had begun in on our lands, "what of those in our village who are bent and disfigured when they first come to the Earth Mother? Does this mean that they are not of good spirit?"

"There is a difference. The situation that I have shared with the both of you is only when a spirit passes through its many seasons with the Earth Mother will this process that I have shared with you apply. The situation that you have shared with me is of another matter."

"When you see another spirit who begins in a deformed way, it is usually for a specific reason. One of these reasons is that this spirit has come in this form because it is the only way that they can learn what they must. The other reason for such things to happen results when a spirit decides, on its own, to end its life path. When they return to the waiting place across the great spirit waters, they see that what they have done was too early. Then they decide that they must return to the Earth Mother for another life path and repeat what they did not learn the first time. It is a way that they have realized the great mistake of ending what they had been given before their time was over, and in this way, they will try to accomplish two life paths worth of learning in one."

"Two Bears," Cheeway asked, sitting much straighter now, "how will we know we are doing the right things that will lead us to the correct path with the Earth Mother?"

Two Bears looked at Cheeway and I and placed a rather large smile on his face and said, "You will both know that you are on the correct path with the Earth Mother when you see the good in all of the change that will be with you."

"But, Two Bears," I said, readjusting my feet below me, "both you and Grandfather have told us that change is a constant in all of our lives. Is this not so?"

"Yes, little one, this is so. To what direction do your speaking words try to take this council?"

"If change is always to be with us, then how will we know the signs that we are given show us the correct path or the wrong one?"

"You are correct when you say that change will always be with all of us. However, it will always be a sign when you can look at the change that has just taken place and see the value of it to you and your spiritual advancement. When you can see the benefit of this change, you will know that you will be on the correct path with the Earth Mother.

"This will be very important to the both of you because as you continue to pass through many seasons with the Earth Mother, you will know that you are preparing yourself in the correct way when all that you will encounter will be seen by you as a lesson to learn from. In this way, when the time comes to meet your other half spirit, you will recognize them for who they are. They will not pass you by as a stranger on the road."

Both Cheeway and I sat in our positions for the next few minutes as we were reflecting on all of the speaking words that Two Bears had shared with us. Periodically, we would catch a glimpse of him out of the corner of our eyes and we could see that he was not in any hurry for us to continue to ask him questions, so we continued to think for awhile longer.

As we thought of which questions that we would ask him from the many that were running through our minds, I looked up at the sky that was resting over our lands and when I did this, I saw two small clouds and they seemed to be racing toward each other.

Their size made me think of two spirits who were looking for each other. I saw that each of these small clouds could do well on their own. But instead of continuing their wandering over our lands separately, they had decided to run to each other and become one. I was thinking how wonderful this sight was as I watched them both come into themselves and become a dark cloud that would bring us the needed water over our lands. I knew that this had happened because they had combined themselves, and as one they would bless all with their life giving waters. Had they continued as two small clouds, the only blessing that would have come to us from them would have been the passing of their shadows over our lands.

Having seen this joining of the two small clouds, I had clearly formed a new question that I wanted to present to Two Bears for his clarification.

CHAPTER 17

❁

Spirit Painting

"Two Bears," I said, bringing my head away from the sky and where I could see Two Bears without difficulty.

"Yes, little one, do you now have a question for me to answer for you?"

"Yes, Two Bears, I do."

"Then go ahead with how you have formed it in your speaking words for me. I am ready now."

"Two Bears," I said, slightly leaning forward in the seated position that I was in. "Both you and grandfather have told Cheeway and I that our other half spirit is walking a life path with us and that they are from the same spirit family as we are from. Is this not so?"

"Yes, both Grandfather and I have seen this in many of our spirit dreams that we have had of both of you."

"Well then, you have also told Cheeway and I that once we have prepared ourselves sufficiently and had learned all of the things that there were to learn, we would be given a choice of returning to the waiting place across the great spirit waters or remaining with the Earth Mother for the rest of the time we had been given. If we would choose to remain with the Earth Mother, then we would recognize our other half spirit for who they were."

"Yes, little one, what you have shared with me so far is very true. You are not mistaking the speaking words that have been shared with you."

"Well, Two Bears," I said, putting my right hand over the side of my face, "if we have prepared ourselves so well and have encountered all of the spirits that will help us on our life path with the Earth Mother, then what will there be left for us to do once we meet our other half spirit?"

Two Bears smiled and looked at me as I finished my speaking words to him. I could tell by the smile that he had placed over his face that he was pleased in what I had asked him. I could not find anything in the speaking words that I had shared with him that should have brought such a level of approval from him.

Finally, Two Bears broke his silence to me and said, "what you will both be able to do for each other will be to keep the other one on the right side of the spirit painting of the life path."

"I looked at Two Bears and I knew that the look that had been placed on my face for him to see could not be mistaken for anything but confusion. I caught a glimpse of Cheeway, who was still sitting next to me. I could see that he too was very confused by the answer that Two Bears had given to my question.

"Two Bears," I said, in a most respectful tone of voice. "I cannot find the answer to the question I asked you in the speaking words that you have shared with me. Could you please make them a little more understandable to us?"

"Yes, little ones, I will do this for you.

"Our people have a very old spirit painting that depicts the way of the life path for two people who walk it together and as one. No one really knows who first created it. Our song legends tell us that it came to these lands of the Earth Mother with us from the times that we shared others with her.

"We have only been able to guess that it may have been left to us by Two Elks and Morning Wind when they became the spirit teachers and guides for our people. However, whoever left this spirit painting for us to learn from has taught us very well on the things that are so necessary for us to learn from.

"In the generations that are on these lands of the Earth Mother's, there is no longer a real painting for us to see. We could only put a copy of the spirit painting into our song legends so that it would be remembered by our people. Those who could learn from it would be able to do so."

"You mean that not everyone can learn from this spirit painting of the past, Two Bears?" Cheeway asked, as he repositioned himself closer to me.

"This is exactly what I am telling you. It is the eyes of the spirit that must see this picture as its form comes to them in the way of the song legends. It is not possible for many who are walking a life path to see this without possessing the spirit eyes of our people.

"It takes a very high level of understanding to be able to understand what this spirit painting has to say. This becomes too difficult for those who only wish to have things handed to them. This is why so very few have been able to relate to a truth such as the one that is placed in the song legend of the spirit painting that I am telling you about."

"Could you tell us about this spirit painting that is in the song legend, Two Bears?" I asked, sitting very erect now in anticipation of hearing a secret truth that not many others knew about.

"Do you both believe that you are ready to embrace its truth, little ones?"

Cheeway and I were nodding our heads in an up and down manner so Two Bears would not mistake our answer to him.

"Very well then, I will tell you about the spirit painting that is contained in our song legend. I believe that you are both ready to hold at least a piece of the understanding that is contained within it.'

"You are correct when you ask what there is left to do when all that has been planned for has been met and worked through. This is a time when the spirit has learned what it originally came among the Earth Mother and her children to learn. However, there is much more to do if a spirit will accept the challenge from those of his spirit group who will come to offer him the choice of returning or staying.

"There is, as you both will come to understand, always more that can be accomplished. This does not only come for your own spirit or for the Earth Mother but for all who have come to her domain. When there is success in any of these quests that will be accomplished, then there are great rewards that will come to those who complete them.

"In most cases though, there will be the need for one additional spirit who will work with you in order to succeed. That additional help will be from your other half spirit. They will be from the spirit family that you are a part of and will either help you from the other side of the great spirit waters or they will join with you in the life path you are walking."

"But, Two Bears," I said, resting my head on both of my palms, "is it not possible to be able to achieve the success of the additional quests alone and without assistance from the other half of ourselves?"

"Initially it would be, little one. However, try to understand that to continue to achieve additional success in further quests alone would be almost impossible because of the great rewards that the Earth Mother will bestow on those who would bring so much to her by their efforts.

"Without the assistance from the other half of your spirit, the possibility of resting on the rewards that have been given to you by the Earth Mother would be just too great. It would seem, to one without any assistance, that after completing only one quest and experiencing the greatness of the rewards that have been given to them, they would believe that this was all that was necessary for them to do…this completion of only one additional quest. Remember that because of the greatness of the rewards that they will receive from the Earth Mother, they could live for the rest of the time that they have in her domain very, very well.

"These rewards are not only of the physical nature, but they also include those things that cannot be touched such as health and well being with yourself and the rest of the world that is around you. So it is, that without the help and reminding from the other half spirit that is from your spirit family, that the chances of only one of these additional quests being accomplished is very high."

"Two Bears," Cheeway said, as he too put his head on both of the palms of his hands, "both you and Grandfather have always told us that it is far better to have only one thing and be happy with it than wish for getting more."

"Very well put, Cheeway. Yes, this is what Grandfather and I have told you both. This is a great truth in the way of understanding the balance of the life path that you are both on. However, this truth must make way for even higher truths once you have accomplished all that you can on your own and you have decided to remain with the Earth Mother for the rest of the time that has been given to you.

"You see, if the domain of the Earth Mother was all in balance, then it would not be necessary for even one additional quest to be performed. However, it is not, so there is much that needs to be done. There will always be so few spirits who will either be willing or capable of performing these additional quests. It becomes very important for those spirits who will reach this point in their advancement to do as many of these additional quests as they can. This is because the Earth Mother and all of her domain are in such need of assistance.

"Remember that all the Earth Mother does is give to us from her love. We will be able to see this when our spirits attain a level of advancement that is sufficient to the level that I am speaking to both of you about. Now, once this understanding comes to each of you, then as you are able to see so many of her loving ways in this life path that you are walking, it will become very clear to both of you how important it is to be able to help her in any way that you can.

"Even when the Earth Mother is filled with the sorrows and hurt that continue to be inflicted upon her and her children, she does not complain. She continues to give all of us her love. When you are able to see this, you will perceive the need to give her as much help as you can. You will be able to see how important it will be to continue to attain as many additional quests as you can.

"So, because of the help that your other half spirit from the spirit group you are a part of gives to you, you will be able to keep a clear mind and heart as you continue to give your assistance to the Earth Mother in more additional quests until the time that has been given to both of you is over. Then you will have no other choice but to rejoin the others of your spirit group in the waiting place across the great spirit waters."

Two Bears paused for another moment and as he did, he turned his head to the western skies that were over our lands.

"Look, little ones, the mirror of the Great Spirit is setting down in his resting place in order to mark the completion of another day for our people. It is time for us to return to our lodges and rest as the children of the Earth Mother will soon be doing."

"But, Two Bears," I said, leaning far forward in my sitting position. "You have not yet told us about the spirit painting that is in the song legend. Is this because you do not believe that either Cheeway or myself are ready for this yet?"

"Not at all, little one. It is only because the time that we have on our lands for this day is over and it is time for the both of you to eat and rest. It is not because I do not believe you are ready to learn of the spirit painting from our song legends."

"Well, when will we be able to learn about this, Two Bears?" Cheeway said, as he was beginning to rock himself in his sitting position.

"I will speak to Grandfather this evening and tell him of the events that I have shared with you. If he wishes, then he will be able to continue at the same point that I have left off from. Will that be alright with the both of you?"

"Will it not be possible for you to continue to share these speaking words with us, Two Bears?" I asked, still sitting in the same position, as was Cheeway now.

"If you both wish to wait until I come back from a long journey that I must begin in the morning, I will be able to continue with these speaking words to both of you. Would you rather wait for my return to hear the rest of the song legend?"

"How long will you be gone, Two Bears?" I asked.

"I should be back before two moons have grown and died on our lands. Will this be too long for the two of you to wait?"

Two Bears could see by the look that we placed on our faces that this would be too long a time to wait to hear the rest of the song legend and looking up at him, we knew that he could read our faces and the meaning that was on them.

"Well then, I can see that both of you consider this to be too long of a time to wait and I can understand this very well. When I was your age, one day could seem like an eternity to me especially when I was waiting for something to come by.

"If you do not mind then, this evening when I pass by Grandfather's house on the way to mine, I will tell him of all the events that I have shared with the both of you and ask him if he would be willing to continue with the speaking words that I did not have the time to finish."

After finishing his speaking words to both of us, Two Bears rose from his seated position, dusting himself off, and walked off into the direction of the village.

Cheeway and I looked at each other and, smiling, we too got up from our seated position on our lands and stretched so that our bodies would know that it was time for them to begin working once again.

"Do you think Grandfather will do as Two Bears asks?" came the stretching voice from Cheeway.

"I believe that if he sees there is to be any value in our learning from this spirit painting, he will Cheeway."

Cheeway stood in front of me nodding his head in an up and down manner to show me that he understood and agreed with the speaking words that I had shared with him.

Taking one last look at the brilliance of the show that the Earth Mother was giving to all who had eyes to see the changing colors of the sunset, we began walking off in the directions of our own homes. We both knew that morning was to come very early for both of us if Grandfather was going to take up Two Bears' request of completing the song legend.

PART VI

❀

A Spirit's Touch

CHAPTER 18

⚘

The Spirit of Silence

The morning on our lands found me lying in my bed asleep. I was awakened by the feeling that someone was standing in the room with me, but lifting my head off of the pillow, I could see that there was no one there and put my head back down once again.

This feeling kept coming to me as I was laying in my bed still half asleep until finally it dawned on me that it was Grandfather who was calling to me from outside of our fence.

Pulling open the curtains on my bedroom window, I could see that both he and Cheeway were sitting in the truck. They were calling to me on this morning and that was what the feeling was all about.

It was considered very rude for any of our people to walk up to the door of the house they did not live in and ask to come in. Grandfather had instructed both Cheeway and myself in the ways of our people that showed us how to use our minds to call to those who were inside of the house in order to receive permission to come onto their lands.

Stumbling out of my bed, I hurried to the front door of our house and motioned to both of them to come into our driveway but quietly because both of my parents were still sleeping. I could see that when I had motioned to Grandfather and Cheeway that they were both laughing, but I could not tell what it was that they saw that was so funny.

Once I was sure that they saw my motion to come onto the land of our house, I went back inside to wash the sleep from myself. As I looked into the mirror that was hanging over the sink, I could see what it was they were laughing at. All of my hair was standing straight up from the top of my head. Somehow, I had gotten very warm last night and because of the water that the body was coating me with and the length of my hair, it looked like someone had scared me.

As I stood in front of the mirror, I could not help but begin to laugh at myself as well. I had to admit that this was a very strange look for me. However, it was one that was going to be corrected with some morning water, soap and a comb.

I finished washing in record time. I knew that the reason Grandfather had come at this hour of the morning was to take Cheeway and myself to another of his special places where he would continue with the speaking words of the song legend about the spirit painting.

Pulling on my pants, shirt, shoes, and a jacket, I left a note where I knew that both of my parents would find it on the front of the ice box. I told them Grandfather and Cheeway had come for me and I was going to be with them for the rest of the day.

Completing the note, I rushed out of the house and into the driveway. I could see that there was still a rather large smile on Grandfather's face. I could tell that he was still remembering the way that I looked when I first came out of the front door to wave them inside of our house's land.

"I must admit," Grandfather said to me, as he was sitting very comfortably behind the steering wheel of his truck, "this is a great improvement over the one that I saw earlier this morning."

I could only smile as I got into the truck. I could tell from the look that was on Cheeway's face that he, too, was trying to hold in his chuckling because of the way that I looked earlier. However, this was not the time to dwell on this and Grandfather started up his truck and backed out of the driveway.

We had been riding in Grandfather's truck for a couple of hours when I realized that he was taking us to a place that was new to both Cheeway and myself. Looking around at the children of the Earth Mother in this land, I could see that not many others had been among them before. I had asked Grandfather where this new place he was taking us was. He only looked at the path that was ahead of him and told me that there were many places that he had not taken Cheeway or myself to before and this was one of them.

As I looked out of the window of the truck we were riding in, I could see that there were places in the side of the mountains that appeared to have many waters and clouds coming out of them. I had asked Grandfather if this was similar to the lands he was taking us to. He only smiled and nodded his head in an up and down manner. I knew that Grandfather had told me all that he was willing to share at this time and had decided not to ask any more questions about where we were going.

I had looked over to the place where Cheeway was sitting to see if he was as curious about this new place as I was but soon discovered that he was fast asleep in the front seat of the truck. With no one left to share speaking words with, I also sat back in my seat and looked for the sleep spirit.

I was suddenly awakened by the stopping of the truck. When I opened my eyes, I was quite delighted to see that Grandfather had brought us to what appeared as a small valley located in the middle of large mountains. In the middle of the valley was a very clear pond and as I looked at it, I could see all the way to the bottom.

Off to the right of the clear pond was a small waterfall which was feeding the small lake, and rolling down my window, I could hear the sounds that it was making as it would breathe in the air that was all around it and take it to the small lake that was below it.

"Hear all the sounds of all the Earth Mother's children," Grandfather said, as he got out of the front of the truck we were in. "In this place, there will be no unnecessary noises. This would disturb the balance that is the Earth Mother."

Hearing these speaking words, Cheeway and I got out of the truck with the utmost of care so we would not cause any imbalance to the Earth Mother or her children on this land of hers.

Grandfather pointed to a small clearing next to the water where he wanted Cheeway and I to set our equipment up. It did not take us very long to take all of the things out of the truck and set them under a leaning shelter that Grandfather had found earlier.

"Who made this small shelter, Grandfather?" I asked, still placing much of the equipment that we had brought with us under it.

"Those who have come here to this place before us," was his answer.

"This is one of the places that the wise of our people come to get their answers to many questions they have about the life path they walk and to ask assistance for others of our people who are having trouble with theirs as well."

"Why did they choose such a place, Grandfather?" Cheeway asked, still setting some of the equipment in place that we had brought with us.

"Because this place of the Earth Mother's allows us to go into and touch the Spirit of Silence when we will need it."

"What does the Spirit of Silence do for us, Grandfather?" I asked, pulling some of the food that we had brought with us out of the burlap sacks that it was packed in.

"The Spirit of Silence does for our spirits the same thing that food does for our bodies. However, one does not see the silence. But believe in me when I tell you that it is very real and necessary for each of us."

"Grandfather," I asked, standing with both of my hands now emptied of equipment and food, "how does this Spirit of Silence work?"

Grandfather looked at both Cheeway and I and made a motion that we should sit on the blankets that we had just spread over the ground beneath us. Sitting down on our blankets, Cheeway and I were very quiet as we waited for him to continue with his speaking words to us on the subject of the Spirit of Silence.

"Before I begin to share further speaking words with the both of you, there is one thing that I would like you to do. I want each of you to close your eyes and listen to the sounds that are around you in this place where we are."

Having always responded to Grandfather's speaking words, Cheeway and I closed our eyes and sat quietly to listen to all of the sounds that were around us. In what seemed to be at least ten minutes, we heard Grandfather's voice call to each of us telling us that it was time for us to open our eyes up and tell him what we heard.

"Well," Grandfather opened the speaking words to us, "what did you hear during this time you had alone?"

"I heard the sound of the waterfall coming into this clear lake that is before us," Cheeway said, holding a very proud look over his face.

"I heard not only the sound of the water coming into the lake, but I heard the sound of the wind spirit calling to the children of the Earth Mother through the many trees that are in this land," I said, looking over at Cheeway to see what his reaction was to my observations.

"Well, that was very good for a beginning," Grandfather said, as he continued looking at both of us. "Tell me now, what else did both of you hear during your short time of silence?"

Both Cheeway and I looked at each other and then turned our heads to look in the direction that Grandfather was sitting. We were sure that Grandfather could see that there was a missing look where there should have been an understanding look that had come over our faces.

"Did either of you hear the sound of the wind rushing past the hawk's wing that is flying above us?"

I looked up from the position that I was sitting in and was surprised to see that there was indeed a hawk flying over us in circular patterns.

"How could you hear such a thing, Grandfather? We did not hear it," I asked, as I continued looking at the form of the hawk over our heads.

"Did either of you hear the breathing of the mountain lion that is circling this place we are in?"

Just as Grandfather finished these speaking words, both Cheeway and I saw the mountain lion's movement through some of the nearby bushes and were very surprised.

"Grandfather," I said, sitting upright in my position, "how is it that you heard so many things that we did not?"

"Little One," Grandfather's speaking words came right back to me, "how is it that you did not?

"One of the reasons that we need to go into the spirit of silence is to learn to listen to all things that are around us. It is from this place that we receive our lessons that will, with the understanding of what it is that they are telling to us, advance our spirits during the life path we are walking with the Earth Mother."

"But, Grandfather," Cheeway said, as he was sitting on his feet, "it does not seem possible to be able to hear all sounds that are around us all of the time."

"No, Cheeway," Grandfather said. looking into the very deep parts of each of us as we were sitting in front of him, "it is not possible to listen to all sounds that are taking place around you. However, you should remember one of the teachings that our people teach to all of the young ones that tells you a person will eventually become the same thing that they think of themselves as being. Well, then this same kind of wisdom applies here in what I am sharing with the both of you.

"It would be of no great importance to be able to hear all of the sounds that were around you. Even if you could, there would be no learning that would benefit you sufficiently because all of your time would be spent in listening so much that there would be no time to learn anything.

"The best advice that I can give to the both of you on this subject is to remind you, that what you think you are, will be what you will become.

"This is the same for going into the Spirit of Silence and learning to listen to those things that are around you. As you become more and more familiar with all that is around you, then it will become clear to you what things are important to you and for the spiritual advancement that you are seeking. Once this becomes clear to you, then you will learn to understand which of the things that are taking place within the domain of the Earth Mother are worth your time and effort of listening to and learning from.

"In this way, you will not be spending great amounts of your time in attaining knowledge that will not serve you and the ends that we are all seeking. Because of this narrowing of your concentration to those things that are of value to each of you, the lessons that are on the outside for you to hear and learn from will benefit you both once you learn how to listen to them. Then your level of understanding will increase accordingly as well.

"In the beginning, you will go into the Spirit of Silence with only one question. That question should be to ask this Spirit of Silence what is it that you can do in order to help others that are around you so that you may help yourself. Over time, and as you become more comfortable with this spirit of the land, you will see that there is great power in silence because it is here that you will find so much of the direction that is necessary to continue in a forward direction to our spiritual advancement.

"When the Spirit of Silence accepts your spirit as a friend accepts another into their house, the learning which will grow understanding will begin. At this point in your life path accomplishments, you will be able to go into the Spirit of Silence with many questions and when you come back, you will be given all of the answers that you are seeking. These answers will guide you in the direction that you must take in order to attain that which you are seeking.

"However, do not make the mistake in thinking that once you have the answers to all of your questions that you are finished and all of the events that need to take place will somehow be done for them. All things that you would like to have done in this life path you are walking will have to be done by you.

"As it is with all things that you will encounter, there is no thing that is ever given that does not have a price to it. If it is an honest thing that you are seeking, then the cost of this will be as well. But there is no case that I have ever seen something given for free."

"Grandfather," I asked, staying seated in the same sitting position that I had started in, "will there ever be a time when we will come back from the Spirit of Silence with answers that are not the correct ones?"

"This will happen when you do not listen to yourself and the questions that you wish to ask before you present yourself to the Spirit of Silence."

I sat back and leaned against one of the large rocks that were with us in this place of sitting and sharing. As I leaned back, I looked up at the tops of the trees that were all around us in the valley we were in. I could see that the wind spirit was carrying its messages from the Earth Mother to her children.

How wonderful, I was thinking, in this place of resting that Grandfather had brought us to. The same laws that applied to our lands would apply here too. This gave me great comfort because I knew that no matter where I would go or what I would learn, that I would not ever be away from those I had come to learn so well. I knew that I would always be close to the Earth Mother, the spirits of the land, and all of her children. I knew that there would not ever come a time when I would not have any of them to speak and share with. I knew this to be true even when I would go into the spirit of silence to search for answers I would need to know.

My restful time here on this land was interrupted by the sound of movement next to me. It was Cheeway, and I could tell by the restless way that he was moving that he was forming a question. Grandfather knew this already and was looking toward him in anticipation of his beginning speaking words to him.

"Grandfather," Cheeway finally called out.

"Yes, Cheeway, what is it?" Grandfather said, sitting on his blanket and trying to hold some of the sunlight out of his eyes. "Do you have a question for me?"

CHAPTER 19

⚜

Knowledge of the Other Spirit
in Joining

Watching this act that was going on between Grandfather and Cheeway was quite humorous. I almost laughed out loud; but when Cheeway looked at me, I decided that now was not the best of times to make fun of his antics.

"Grandfather, you told us that you would continue with the speaking words that Two Bears had begun for us. Can you do this for us now?"

"Yes, I can do this, but before I begin I would like both of you to tell me, in your own words, just how much Two Bears shared with you so that I may better understand where I should begin."

"But, Grandfather," Cheeway continued, "did not Two Bears tell you himself where he had left the last of his speaking words?"

"Yes, Cheeway, Two Bears did tell me, but I would like to hear it from your own words. In this way, I can tell how much you did and how much you did not understand of the story that he told you."

Cheeway and I looked at each other for the next few moments. We were discussing with each other all of the events that Two Bears had shared with us. We wanted to show Grandfather how much we really did understand so our efforts that we were making on this subject were great ones...at least they were to us.

We took turns repeating Two Bears' speaking words and as we continued with our recounting, we could see that Grandfather had placed a large smile on his face. We knew that we were doing very well with remembering the steps of events that Two Bears had shared with us, and Grandfather was very pleased.

It did not take us as long as we had anticipated to tell all of the things that Two Bears had shared with us. When we finished, we both sat back against the rocks that were behind us to take a small rest from such an intense encounter with our memories.

"Very good, little ones," Grandfather said, as his smile grew across his face. "It is always so reassuring to see that not all of your memories are tuned into playing with the Earth Mother's children. It is good to know that some of it has been set aside for important things.

"Well then, where would be a good place to start, I wonder?" finishing his speaking words to us, Grandfather was looking right through the both of us. We could see that he was looking for some kind of an answer to his question.

"Why not start at the place where we left off?" Cheeway said, pulling himself away from the rock and toward the position where Grandfather was seated.

"Yes, I believe that this would be a good place to begin.

"Come closer to me, little ones. We do not want to disturb the balance of the Earth Mother with our voices being louder than they should be, do we?"

Cheeway and I pulled ourselves up and scooted across the sitting blankets that were underneath us. We had repositioned ourselves almost at a place where Grandfather's feet were when we noticed that he was making a motion with his right hand that we had come close enough for what he was going to share with us.

Being in the place where all three of us were comfortable, we sat and waited to hear the speaking words Grandfather would share with us about the spirit painting. Grandfather took a large breath, and closing his eyes for just a moment, we could tell that he was clearing his thoughts so that he could devote all of his energies to telling us the remainder of the song legend.

"The events that Two Bears told the both of you are very accurate and they hold great truths inside of them. He was also correct when he told you that for generations, our people have believed that it was Two Elks and Morning Wind that originally gave us the spirit painting. I believe that our ancestors were correct.

"Two Bears explained to you that it takes both you and your other half spirit to continue forward with the additional quests that will be offered to you by the Earth Mother. This is because of the greatness of the rewards that will be given to those who will complete even one quest successfully. He told you how important it was to understand how much a spirit from your spirit family is needed to keep you on the correct path when you are finally at this stage of your advancement, did he not?"

"Yes, he did, Grandfather. But there is one question that I would like to ask you about now if that would be alright with you," I said, trying to be as serious as I could be.

"And what would that question be, little one?" Grandfather said, leaning towards my position on the sitting blanket.

"I am becoming confused with a term that both you and Two Bears have used in your descriptions of our other half spirit, Grandfather. I do not want to carry this confusion with me."

"And what is it that is confusing you?" Grandfather said, taking on a more sincere look about him.

"Is this other half spirit the other half of us, or is it a spirit from our own spirit family, or is it a spirit we are married to from across the great spirit waters."

"I can see how this would confuse anyone. Yes, let me take some time and explain in the speaking words of our ancestors what these differences are so it will become easier to understand.

"It is true that we each have another half of ourselves walking a life path with the Earth Mother at the same time that we are. However, this is not the other half spirit that Two Bears and I have been telling you both about. While it is true that they are one half of us, it is also true that they are also the complete opposite of ourselves. This would make it almost impossible to get along with them. The reason that they are in existence is to balance out our learning. We should not encounter them until we have crossed the great spirit waters. When we arrive at the waiting place, there they will be and we will come into one another once again. From all that both of our half spirits have learned will come the true advancement that will lead us forward to the Great Spirit. Remember, this other half spirit of yours can only advance as far and as fast as you do. However, it was not ever the intention of either the Great Spirit or the Earth Mother that we should ever meet them when we are walking a life path here.

"The spirit that we have referred to both of you as being your other half comes from the last two observations that you have shared with me. They will either be from your spiritual family or they will be one to whom you are closely tied to from your spiritual family.

"In both cases, these other half spirits will be of such great help to you that each of you will wonder how you could have ever done anything at all without each other."

"Grandfather," I said, still sitting in my attentive position on my sitting blanket, "could you tell us a little more about the difference between these two kinds of spirits?"

"Yes, but I must not take too much time on this subject because we are getting away from the original purpose of our being here in this land of balance.

"There are many different levels of closeness among our spiritual families. First, you must realize that there is no man or woman spirit, there is only a spirit. Each spirit is so complete that there is no need to be one or the other. So when we come to the Earth Mother to walk a life path with her, we come here as either a man or a woman and this is because of the lessons that we can learn in one role or the other.

"When you meet one of the spirits from your spiritual family, you will see them as a female, that is if they are the one that you were destined to come into contact with. Both of you will have made this arrangement before either of you entered into the domain of the Earth Mother's. Both of you will have set many lessons before yourselves so that you will be able to balance each other out more completely.

"When one is weak in one area of understanding or learning, the other one will be very strong and will not mind sharing their strengths with the other one. Because of all of the events that you both have been through, you will find that neither one of you will ever misuse the other one nor will you take them for granted. As a matter of fact, you will find yourself getting closer to each other in ways that are well beyond anything that you have ever encountered before.

"In the beginning, you will meet many others who are walking with the Earth Mother. You will find that there will be a certain level of excitement that comes from the newness of another with whom you will become physically attached. This newness is a very good thing, or so you will think. However, as time for the both of you continues and you each become more familiar with each other's bodies and their ways, you may find that this newness is wearing away and is not being replaced with anything else to take its place.

"As this happens, you will find that each of you will become tired of the other one. When this happens, it is the best thing to say your farewells. If you do not say your farewells then, well…eventually you will very likely become very strong enemies. One of the major pastimes that will follow then will be spending your time finding ways to hurt the other one because you feel that they have left you completely without any kind of love in your life.

"I have known some who have spent their entire life path with someone like this. Believe me, there was nothing learned and I know that when they returned back across the great spirit waters to the waiting place, they found that they had put up with so much bad and for no reason. They will become very saddened to find that they received no gain from their life path. And all of the lessons that they had set before themselves in order to advance their own spirit have been missed. What is even a greater sadness is that if they wish to relearn these lessons to gain a better understanding of things that they will need to advance their own spirits, then they will have to do it all over again. This is a very difficult thing for any spirit to have to do and I would not recommend this path for either of you.

"It will be from meeting those others who will come to you and those who you will come to that will begin to prepare you for the one who you will both eventually find. It is by sharing with others that we will find the truer meaning of what it will take to see through this newness of being with another. Do not take this lightly though. The worst thing that you could ever do in this process is to hurt another while you are learning. There are the kinds of hurts to the spirit that can last for many lifetimes, so be very careful when you are with others in this way. Make sure that before you cause them hurt in any way that you pick up your sleeping blanket and leave. These kinds of hurts that you might cause a spirit will not only follow them, but they will follow you as well and it requires great work to heal them.

"As you travel through more and more seasons with the Earth Mother and gain understanding of yourself and what your needs are, it eventually becomes more clear to you what you are looking for and needing in another person. You will understand that there will be many areas within yourself that you cannot work on and you will consider them to be weaknesses. You will understand that there are many areas within yourself that you know very well and you will consider them to be your strengths.

"As you go forward through these seasons of change and understanding, you will find another who will come into your life that will meet these weaknesses and will need these strengths that you possess. You will find that this makes you happy and it also makes you become cautious as well.

"You will have learned, from the other experiences, that this might not be what you have been looking for. So you sit back within yourself and observe this other person that has just come into your life.

"As you observe them, you find that there is much more to them than you had found in the others that had come into your life. You will notice as you continue with your observations, that they too are observing you as well. However, neither of you is finding anything that is remotely unfamiliar about the other one. It is like finding parts of an old friend who is now with you. Before you know it, what was once your shell of protection, that you had built around yourself, is coming down and all by itself. You will find that not only does the physical portion of your new found other half excite you but you find that many things that you will discuss will cause you to think and understand more of the nature of the life path you are walking with the Earth Mother.

"When both of you discuss your feelings, you will find that there will be nothing that is different from what the other one is feeling or thinking. When you each discuss the events that have happened to each of you, you will both not see them as anything that is bad…you will each see them as being the very things that have created each of you into the one that they are, and it is who they are that you need.

"Now, the difference between meeting the other half of your spirit that is from your spiritual family and the one to whom you are very closely associated with from across the great spirit waters is this. The one who is from your spiritual family will have to go through as many experiences as you did in order to come to you. But the one spirit to whom you are connected with in your spiritual family many come to you without having gone through any of the events that you did. Those who meet this spirit while walking a life path with the Earth Mother meet them because they have been given a great chance to receive the blessings of rest during the life path they are walking. The reward of their quests are great and all who come into contact with both of them will feel their greatness of love and this will bless them greatly.

"However, for the both of you, the other half of your spirit will be from our spiritual family. This is necessary because of all of the things that there are to do for the Earth Mother and her children. Because of this union that is in the seasons ahead of both of you, you will become very familiar with all of the spirits of the land and they will instruct you in their ways.

"Has this answered your question, little one?" Grandfather asked, as he looked in my direction.

"Yes, Grandfather, it does," I answered.

PART VII

❀

Journey Through the Spirit Painting

CHAPTER 20

❁

Return to the Spirit Painting

Grandfather looked at us and slowly raised his right hand so the palm was held in a downward position. "Look at all that is around you," he said, as he continued waving his arm in a circular manner. "All that you see before you has started out at the point that we will need to be before we can come to understand what the spirit painting is all about.

"All of the children of the Earth Mother know what it is that they must do. They all know just how many seasons they have to complete it in. They also know that when they have completed their quests, that any time that is left to them will be given to them for their enjoyment.

"We, on the other hand, must go through many seasons and experiences in order to reach this same point that I am talking about. This is where the spirit painting that I believe that Two Elks and Morning Wind have left for us comes from. The message to us carries a warning to us on what might happen once we meet our other spirit half in this life path we are walking if we are not careful."

"Grandfather," I said, sitting straighter than usual, "what do you mean when you tell us that the message is not the one that would seem to be the most obvious?"

"What I mean is just that. The spirit painting shows a man and a woman standing in three different places on it. There is one picture of them standing on the left of the painting, one in the middle of it, and one on the right of it. Now, this is what the song legends lead us to believe and I have no reason to think otherwise.

"First, the man and woman who are standing on the left side of this painting show to us how they would live if they lived on this side of the life path together. The left side of the spirit painting shows us that this is the place where the individual is placed before all other things. In this place, it is one's self that is put before all other things and because of this, their life path together will not be good.

"In this place of the spirit painting, is where two people joined together for their life path will always think of themselves first. This results in each of them always feeling very sorry and sad for themselves no matter what the other one will do. In this stage of the life path that is painted on the spirit painting, is where nothing will ever go right for either of them. They will always be trying to satisfy the other one not realizing that no thing can ever satisfy them while they are in this stage of the spirit.

"While they each stay on this side of the spirit painting, they will always feel that all things that happen are happening only to them. They cannot see the goodness of things because they can only see the sadness that they have created around them. They do not realize that this sadness that they have created has come from their own minds and it has no bearing in their real world.

"On this side of the spirit painting, there will be a loud cry from within themselves. These voices, and they do believe that they are real, are coming from the emotional side of their life path. They will seem to guide and tell them many things that are taking place not only with the other one that they are joined to, but also with regard to all others they come into contact with.

"These voices that come to them are coming from within their emotional side of their spirit. Because this is where they are coming from, they will not ever be correct. The emotional side of ourselves is only there so we can feel things, but it does not understand anything at all.

"This emotional voice that comes to those who stand on the left side of the spirit painting is most always giving them the wrong kind of advice. Each time they listen to it, and react to it, the worse things will become for them and all who are connected to them.

"Eventually, they will focus all blame for actions that they have caused to occur on the other one that they are with. In time, not even the one who they have joined with can bring them back. Within a matter of years, because of all the negative living that they have done, they will take on the appearance of one who has many more seasons to their life path than they really do and their health will not be good either.

"The spirit painting shows us that for those who will stand on the left of it, that they will not ever realize the benefits of spiritual growth. They are so concerned with what they will receive in the life path that they are walking that they do not see anything else. Because of this, they will pull others into this place with them when allowed. This will stop all that will come to them from attaining any spiritual growth as well.

"Because there is no spiritual growth, they will always feel that there is something missing in their life path. They will spend the rest of the time that has been given to them in a continual search for what that something is. However, this search will not ever end until they learn how to move themselves from the left side of the spirit painting to the right of their position.

"If they do not move all the way to the right of the spirit painting, then they will have more trouble than they did originally.

"This is where the second portion of the spirit painting shows the same two people standing in the middle. You see, in the middle of the painting is a very dangerous position. It is not on the left and it is not on the right.

"When the two people have been on the left and make their attempt of removing themselves to the right, they usually make the mistake of thinking that they are on the right of the spirit painting, when in fact they have only traveled to the middle of it.

"It can become very confusing to those who are traveling within these limitations. As our song legends tell us, any movement toward the right of the spirit painting will teach valuable lessons. However, our ancestors have also told us that to stop any kind of movement within this truth is dangerous.

"Now, the middle of the spirit painting is a place where there is no commitment of any kind. By not making any commitment, those who are in this place will come to believe that they are actually making progress because nothing bad has been done.

"Take, for example, the two who were once on the left side of the spirit painting. When they get to the middle of the painting, they are no longer thinking so much of themselves all of the time. The voices from their emotional side of their spirit are not coming to them as frequently as they were while they were on the left side. This fools them into thinking that their progress has been sufficient and that they are now standing on the right side of the painting. But in truth, they are in a place that is perhaps more dangerous and can do more harm than the one they just left.

"This second place is called the place of nothingness. It is here that to do nothing will make one feel as though they are proceeding forward, that their spiritual advancement is being met. They become so convinced of this that they go out of their way to keep others who are around them from doing nothing at all as well. It is from this place where they will most likely do more hurt to others because they will try to convince them that to find security is the most important thing for them. They will try to convince others that to look for opportunity is dangerous…but our teachings tell us that this is the way to growth and learning.

"While they were on the left side of the painting, they were only causing spiritual harm to themselves and perhaps a few others. However, when they are in the middle of the spirit painting, they will become so convinced that their way is the only path by which anyone should walk that it will become their sole quest to make sure that as many others as they can possibly come into contact with will do exactly as they are doing.

"Another reason that this position on the spirit painting becomes so dangerous is that while they were on the left side, they could feel. When they were hurt, they could see that there was something wrong with what they were doing.

"However, when they are stuck in the middle of the spirit painting, they will perceive those others who do not have as many difficulties as they do as being ones who have not yet discovered their truth. They will begin a tireless quest to help these others who are not as burdened with problems as they are to become like them. Otherwise, in their minds, those others might do something wrong.

"Those who get stuck in the middle will not see others who do not have the same kinds of problems as they do as doing anything right. They will see them as being uninformed and they will try everything possible to inform them and pull them to where they are.

"There is much harm done from those who remain in the middle because of this. The spiritual harm that is done by them will often set them back greatly and it will affect those who they are able to convince in a very negative way as well.

"In any case, the left side of the spirit painting creates no spiritual advancement. All the spirits who walk there will have to repeat their lessons over again. The ones who walk in the middle of the spirit painting will not only have to do their life path over again, but they may even lose what advancement they had made prior to coming to the Earth Mother because of the great harm they will cause to the other spirits who have listened to them."

"Grandfather," both Cheeway and I said at the same time, "how will we ever know when we are in such a place?"

"You will know these places when all of the things that you will try to accomplish are met with failure and resistance. You will know when you are in one of these two places when you find that your only concern will be in receiving and not in returning from what has been given to you. You will know these places by looking carefully on the others who associate with you and the ones that you associate with.

"Whenever you are in either of these two places that have been shown to us in this spirit painting, you will find that things will not be happy. The only joy you will find in either of these places will be in knowing that when one day has passed that you will have one day less to spend on the life path you are walking."

"This is a very sad path to walk, Grandfather," I said, sitting with my shoulders almost on my knees. "How is it that these spirits do not know that where they are is so bad? Can they not see what they are doing to themselves and those others who they have come into contact with?"

"This is the truth of what I have been sharing with the both of you. They cannot see what it is that they are doing. In their eyes, all of the things that they do to themselves and others is what they see as the best for all concerned."

"But, Grandfather," Cheeway said, sitting on the back portion of his legs now, "can they not feel the difference from those bad things that they are doing?"

"It is like I have told both of you. They do not know any difference. They have done all that they believe that is necessary for the advancement of their spirit but in truth, they have not ever allowed their spirit out of their bodies. They do not have the ears and eyes of the spirit so they cannot see or hear those things they do. They will not accept help from others either. This will only cause them to try to change you as well.

"Let me put it to both of you in this way," Grandfather said, putting on a large smile over his face. We knew that he had found a way of simplifying things for us to understand and this was pleasing him greatly.

"Think of ice cream. You both like this, don't you?"

Grandfather saw that we were both shaking our heads in an up and down manner and rather quickly. We knew that there would be no doubt in his mind that we both liked this and from his experience of buying some of it for both of us, he also knew that we did not ever receive our fill of it either.

"Well, before you knew of ice cream, you did not miss it at all, did you?"

"Well, no…" Cheeway said, placing a puzzled look over his face.

"It is the same for those who are stuck on the left or the middle of the spirit painting, that I have been telling you about. Since there is not one of them who has ever experienced the right side of the painting, then they do not miss it because they do not know any better."

Grandfather allowed his speaking words to trail off for a few moments as he looked into each of us to ensure himself that we did understand what it was that he was saying.

"Well, Grandfather," Cheeway said, sitting a little more erect now, "why does not someone just offer them some ice cream so they can know the difference?"

"It is my greatest hope that the life path that both of you are on will be able to do just that kind of a thing without becoming lost as they are," Grandfather said, turning his head into the direction of the waterfall that was behind the both of us.

"I will pray to the Great Spirit that you both will be of sufficient strength to be able to understand that not all of those who you will encounter will like ice cream."

"What will we do when we encounter those spirits who will not listen to what we will tell them, Grandfather?" I asked, sitting very still so I could receive each speaking word that he was going to share with us.

"You must move on to the next ones, little ones. The seasons that are given to each of us by the Earth Mother do not give us the possibility of being able to spend too much time on any one spirit. You will find some who will accept what you have to share with them, and for those you will become very happy. You will find those who will not accept those things that you will wish to share with them and this will make you very sad. However, keep in mind that because you know these things, you must not ever force them on others no matter how much you would like to. It must always be left to their own choice as to what they will accept and what they will reject.

"This is a very great lesson in truth that I share with both of you. It is the wise and understanding spirit who only offers truth to others. It is the very negative spirit who tries to force their truth onto others."

"Grandfather," I said, "what of the third portion of the spirit painting? How will we know when we are on this side of it?"

"When you and the one you finally will join with are together, you will find that there will be nothing that happens to either of you that will not give you both continued advancement of the spirit. When you are both there, you will find that there will not be anything that will come before you that you cannot understand. You will find that you will understand the importance of putting the other one before you and your needs. You will know the benefits and spiritual growth that result from doing this. When you are both in the right side of the painting, you will understand what it means to touch each other's spirit freely and nothing that will ever be shared by the two of you will be held with a closed hand. Rather, it will be with an open one...one that will give the freedom of spirit that is needed for the both of you to grow."

Grandfather looked at Cheeway and I with a look in his eyes that held a twinkling for the both of us. "Yes, I can see the both of you being in this place that is on the right side of the spirit painting. I can feel some of the joy that you are both yet to know. I can see great spiritual growth from this life path that you are both walking."

Grandfather paused for a brief moment, then said, "This is good, all that I see of your seasons to come."

CHAPTER 21

❀

Feeling the Spirit of Silence

There was a silence that fell over all three of us after Grandfather had finished sharing his speaking words with us. Both Cheeway and I could see that, for some reason that was not known to either of us, he had taken on a large weight to himself, and we could see that in the position that he was sitting, that its presence was also known to us.

However, as Grandfather sat in this position of his, he was smiling at the both of us and making a motion with his right hand over the small valley that we were in. We could tell that he wanted us to go into the spirit of silence so that we could hear the sounds that are made by the Earth Mother, the spirits of the land, and all of her children when there has been established a balance that we are all striving for within ourselves.

For the next hour or so, we all went into the spirit of silence. Grandfather went into this to find some of the answers that he was looking for, and Cheeway and I went in to acquaint ourselves with another friend that he had introduced to us. For us, this was new, but we could feel that soon we would know more.

Having gone into the silence, I was allowing myself to float on the very top of the crystal clear lake that was next to our sitting positions. I was feeling what it was like to be a small wind spirit speaking to the life that was around me. As my mind was becoming quite accustomed to this new world that Grandfather had introduced us to, I felt a presence of someone standing next to me.

I became startled and jumped from the position that I was in, to turn myself around in order to see who had been able to walk up behind me. When I turned around to see who was standing there, I was surprised to find that the space was only filled by the air.

When I looked over to the position where Cheeway had been sitting, I discovered that I had turned around so quickly that he had also become stunned by this sudden movement. Instead of being in the last position that I remembered him being in, he was laying across Grandfather's feet where I had knocked him into and was looking at me with eyes as wide as the night owls.

"Do not be frightened, little ones, you only felt one who was coming to visit you...that is all. While you do not know them yet, in a few seasons, you will come to know them very well."

Finishing these speaking words to us, Grandfather made a motion to both of us that we should begin to pack all of our equipment up and set it in the back of the truck. The day was getting long now and we would all be expected back in our homes.

Cheeway and I did not waste any time in putting all of our things back into the truck.

"Do not forget to wave your farewells to those who live with the Earth Mother in this place. Let them know how much you enjoyed visiting them in their home," came Grandfather's words to us, as we climbed into the front of the truck.

We did as he asked of us and feeling the truck begin to pull itself out of the small valley we had been in gave us a great feeling of relief. We knew that soon, we would be back among those things that we felt, but we knew it would be with more understanding than we had now.

As we pulled out of the valley, my mind was running over the speaking words that Grandfather had shared with me. "They were only coming to visit you. You do not know them now, but in a few seasons, you will come to know them very well."

These speaking words were running through my mind as we left the small valley. I could still feel that feeling of surprise that I received when I felt someone behind me and turned to find that there was no one there at all.

I could only hope that when it did come my time to meet them, whoever they were, that I would be as full of the spirit of calmness as Grandfather was when he explained to me.

PART VIII

❀

THE SPIRIT LIGHTS

CHAPTER 22

❀

What Spirits Leave Behind

It had been several days since Grandfather had shared the rest of the song legend about the spirit painting with us. The speaking words that Two Bears and Grandfather had shared with us created a great weight to our learning. We had been using these past few days to gain a little more insight into the meaning of them, so that in time, we would be able to understand them more completely.

Grandfather and Two Bears would tell us that all of the speaking words that they would share with us in our youth would become very necessary for us in order to complete the quests that would come to us in our life path with the Earth Mother.

Cheeway and I would often speak to each other of these events and try to come up with additional ways to increase our levels of understanding. We did not want to go through all of the seasons of our life path and not be able to recognize our other half spirit.

I was sitting under the small pine tree that we had rescued in some of the mountains near our village. I was thinking of these events that had happened to both of us over the past few days. My mind was brought out of its thinking by the sounds of someone calling my name.

Turning around to see who it was, I saw Cheeway standing at the entrance to our house's land. He looked rather excited as he was calling to me so I walked over to him to see what was wrong.

"Cheeway," I said, "you have the look of a frightened rabbit. What has happened to you that gives you this look?"

Trying to catch his breath and form his speaking words to me, I could see that Cheeway's eyes had seen something that had truly frightened him.

"I have just walked through the old part of the village and have seen them," Cheeway said, as he was still trying to control his breathing enough so that he could pass his speaking words through it.

"Who did you see, Cheeway?" I asked, as I put my right hand on his left shoulder.

"The ones Grandfather and Two Bears have told us about," came the reply out of Cheeway's open mouth.

"Do you mean Two Elks and Morning Wind, Cheeway?"

"Yes, I think this is who I saw," Cheeway said, turning his head from the direction to where he was looking and focusing on me. "They spoke to me."

"What did they say, Cheeway?"

"They said that they would be back for me and one other."

I could tell that Cheeway was badly in need of something that would calm him down before he would go on sharing his speaking words with me. So, grabbing him by the left arm, I took him inside of my parents' house where we could share something cold to drink from our ice box.

After a few moments, Cheeway was looking more relaxed and I decided to continue with the set of questions to him that had formed in my mind.

"Where were you when this event happened to you, Cheeway?" I asked him, handing him another glass of water.

"I was at the site of the ancient village on the mesa."

"What were you doing there, Cheeway?" I asked, looking at him, trying to see the kind of things that Grandfather so often looked for in each of us between his speaking words.

"I was looking at the place where the old ones once lived. I went there to see if my mind could see what their village looked like. When I did this, I heard a voice calling my name. This voice seemed to be coming from all around me because each time that I would turn my head around, it would seem as though it was coming from each direction that I was looking.

"Suddenly, as the voice had repeated my name to me several times, there came a bright white light and it was shining directly in front of me. In the beginning, I thought that those who were in the waiting place were coming for me, but just when I thought that, the light went away and told me that they would be back for me and one other."

I could see that the look Cheeway had put over his face was sincere and frightened. I decided that the only way that we would be able to understand this was to go to Grandfather's house and share Cheeway's experience with him. Telling Cheeway about this, he sat in the kitchen chair and could only shake his head in an up and down manner to tell me that he agreed with what I had just told him.

We did not waste any time in leaving my parents' kitchen and before we could even hear the back door close behind us, we were already out of the gate that led into the house's land. I do not recall if we were running or just walking very fast, but it was only about three minutes before we were standing at Grandfather's gate and calling to him.

"Do you think he is home?" Cheeway asked, echoing a shaking in his voice.

"I hope that he is, Cheeway. But if he is not at his home, then we can sit by the fence and wait for him. What do you think?"

"I think that this is a very good idea. At least here, I feel a little better."

"I think that it is the spirits who live here with Grandfather, Cheeway. They must like us and are trying to help us as much as they can."

Just as I finished speaking to Cheeway, we heard two voices speaking to each other from around the corner. One of the voices we recognized as Grandfather and the other one we knew was Two Bears. They were speaking of things that were bringing them happiness and we could hear them laughing between sharing their speaking words with each other.

Just as they rounded the corner, they saw both of us sitting at the gate. When they saw us and the look that was on both of our faces, they hurried to the position where we were both seated. Getting to our positions, they both squatted on the ground with us and immediately began feeling our faces and necks thinking that something was physically wrong with us.

As I looked over at where Cheeway was sitting, I saw that he was looking worse. He was dripping with sweat from all over his head. All of the places where the sweat was coming from him was turning into mud as it met the dust that was on us both.

Grandfather asked me if I was alright. I told him that I was but that it was because of how Cheeway was feeling that we were here.

Grandfather asked me to tell him all of the events that had taken place with Cheeway that I could remember. I hurriedly told him all of the things that had happened since Cheeway found me by the gate of our house. I told him about the voices that Cheeway told me he heard and the light that came to him as well.

Hearing this account of events, both Grandfather and Two Bears put a look of great surprise on their faces. I could tell that what I had told them had a great weight…a weight that for whatever reason Cheeway was carrying and all by himself.

Cheeway had been laid on the floor of Grandfather's house. It seemed to be a very comfortable place. Next to it was the fire place and we had shared many fond memories there. Two Bears had left the house in a hurry. When I asked Grandfather where Two Bears was running off to, he told me that Two Bears had just gone out to get a few people that would be needed for Cheeway to get better.

Grandfather sat next to Cheeway on the floor now and was rubbing some kind of a white paste over his chest. Cheeway was no longer awake and I thought that he was asleep–for awhile–because of his being tired.

"Is Cheeway just resting, Grandfather?" I asked, standing next to their position.

"For the time being, little one, he is resting. However, we must perform some of the things that our ancestors have taught to us in order for Cheeway to get better."

"But, Grandfather, Cheeway is not sick. Do you think that he is just pretending in order to fool all of us?"

"I do not believe that even Cheeway could pretend so well. He is not sick as you know the word, but he is in trouble with his spirit and we need to help him."

That was the last of the speaking words that Grandfather was willing to share with me on this night. After that, he began holding his hands over Cheeway's head and chest and was singing a spirit caller's song.

As I sat down on the dirt floor of the house, I knew that I should not interrupt him with any of my questions that I had at this time. I could tell that Grandfather was very deep within himself by the tone of voice that he was singing this spirit caller's song with over Cheeway. I knew if I would even make a small noise, it would interrupt the medicine that Grandfather was trying to work on Cheeway.

Not wanting to do this, I rose from my sitting position as quietly as I could and walked out the front door. I only knew that I did not want anything to happen to Cheeway. I felt that the best place for me at this time would be on the outside of the house where I could sit and listen to the spirit caller's song that Grandfather was singing over Cheeway.

I had found a nice place to sit. It was next to the front door of the house and was supported by a couple of large pieces of wood that seemed to support my back, as a friend would do. I felt better in this position. When I looked up from where I had seated myself, I could still see into the house even though the screened door was closed.

As I sat there listening to words that Grandfather was singing over Cheeway, I knew that this problem was not a light one. As I would follow the singing words of Grandfather's, I could also feel his full range of emotion. He would go from sad to happy, from asking to telling and so it went. I did not ever remember a time when he would ever show so much emotion for anything that we had happen to either of us.

My concentration was interrupted by the sounds of many feet running in the direction of the house. I turned my head and could see that it was Two Bears with several others from our village. Each of them had something in their hands and when they reached the house, they did not even notice me sitting there. They went directly into his house.

Within a few moments, all of the windows and doors flew open and all that was taking place within the entire house was now very visible to me. I could see that Grandfather and Two Bears were each standing over Cheeway. There were many others around different portions of his house singing and playing flutes, rattles, and drums.

I could not remember when Grandfather's house ever had so many people in it. I could not ever remember when Cheeway had ever really been sick. I could not ever remember feeling so bad myself because my best friend was very sick and there was nothing that I could do about it.

So, I continued to sit there in my place just to the outside of the house wishing that someone would be kind enough to tell me just what was going on with my best friend. These thoughts of not knowing were weighing very heavy on me and I found that there were small streams of water coming out of my eyes. However, I did not want to make any noise because it might disrupt what Grandfather and Two Bears were trying to do for Cheeway and I did not want to disturb the spirit drums that were beating by the others of our village. They were doing this so Grandfather and Two Bears could travel into the spirit and help Cheeway.

CHAPTER 23

❊

The Old Woman

As I was sitting there in the place that was by the front door, I suddenly felt a hand touch my left shoulder. Turning around, I saw that it was an old woman but due to the poor light out in the front yard, I could not make out her face. I could only guess that she had come with the others that Two Bears brought with him. In any case, I could feel nothing but kindness that was coming from her so I turned back into the direction of the house where I could see all that was going on inside.

"You know why they have opened all of the windows and doors, don't you?" came the voice of the old woman from behind me.

"No, I do not know this reason. Do you?" I asked, still staring into the house where all of the work was being performed over Cheeway.

"It is so that if either Grandfather or Two Bears must travel with their spirit to the outside of the house, then they will not find any restrictions to their coming and going. It is also necessary because they are calling on many spirits from the great waiting place because they need their help."

This old woman seemed to be quite knowledgeable about the events that were taking place within the house. Her voice did not seem to be as old as her body was, but perhaps it was because the sound of it was so kind and understanding that it was all that I wanted to hear and know. I knew that I very much needed her kind and gentle sound giving to me. So, I decided to continue listening to her while I watched all of the events that were taking place within the house.

"You do not need to be frightened, little one," the old woman told me.

"Why do you call me little one? No one but Grandfather and Two Bears calls me that and it is only when Cheeway and I are together."

"But you are still a little one. The name that I am referring to you is one that has been set aside for all of our children. It is a way of showing affection in the speaking words that we will share with them. Will you allow me to share speaking words with you? I will tell you that they will only help you in this time of need that you have."

Since I only felt a goodness and a caring from this old woman, I continued to sit there looking into the house and shook my head in an up and down motion so that she would know that it would be alright with me.

"Very well then, we shall share speaking words on this night. I believe that you have a great many questions that you are wondering about. If you would like, you could ask them of me and I might be able to answer them for you."

Both the old woman and I did not leave our positions as we continued sharing our speaking words with each other. I did not feel as though she was offended, because for some reason, I felt that she knew how important it was that I keep my sight on the position where Cheeway was laying on Grandfather's floor.

"What has happened to Cheeway?" I asked, with a very emotional voice to the old woman.

"He has walked across a place in one of our older villages where no goodness lives. This is what has happened to him," came the reply from the old woman.

"What do you mean? I have not ever heard of such places that are of our people," I said, still looking into the house where Cheeway was lying.

"You are very correct in what you say to me, little one. However, these two who teach you cannot be expected to be able to share all knowledge with the both of you in this short time they have left with the Earth Mother. One could only hope that for the time that is remaining that they will find the time that is necessary to share those things that will benefit each of you the most."

"Well, I did not ever think of it in this way. But what you tell me in the speaking words that you are sharing with me is that the time that is left for Grandfather and Two Bears is not for much longer. Do you mean that they, too, will leave us soon?" I said to the old woman, leaving a trace of sadness in the tone of voice that I was using.

"There will be the time that is necessary to instruct the both of you in the ways of our people. You will find, though, as you each pass through more and more seasons with the Earth Mother, that when someone is no longer walking a life path with her that they are not gone from you at all. You only have to learn how to speak in a completely different way though in order to continue to be with them."

"Old woman," I said, still not taking my eyes off from the position where Cheeway was laying on Grandfather's floor, "you are now telling me of things that Grandfather and Two Bears have touched on with the speaking words that they have shared with me. If I do not understand your words completely, can I tell you?"

"Of course you can, little one. This is one of the reasons that I am here with you on this night of your need."

There was something in the tone of her voice that gave me the feeling that she had come to this place where I was sitting only for me. Somehow, I had the feeling that her only purpose in being here was to give me comfort. However, I knew that this was a very foolish way to think because it was not me who was in trouble but it was Cheeway. For me to think of anything else, in my mind, would be to take away from Cheeway some of the attention and help that he needed. So, I allowed this thought to fall away from me and to concentrate on what I was able to see within the house while I continued to share speaking words with the old woman.

"Old woman," I said, "can you tell me more about this thing that has happened to Cheeway?"

"Very well," the old woman said. "Where would you like me to begin for you?"

"Anywhere I could understand more of what has happened to him so that neither one of us will ever make such a mistake again," I said, putting my head on my knees that were under them now.

"Perhaps the best way for me to explain this to you is to share a picture with you first. Have you ever seen the waters of the river that runs close to your village when there has not been any rain or storms in this land?"

"You mean the Rio Grande?" I said, feeling a little confused as to why she did not know the name of the waters that flowed across our lands.

"Yes, this is the one that I mean. Have you noticed how on even the calmest of days that there is always some of the bad things that the river does not want sitting on the shore or next to it?"

"Yes, Grandfather has told us often that to drink from these places is not very good for us at all and that we should always avoid these kinds of places. He has told us that this is where the river is cleansing itself."

"Very good, little one. Well, it is the same way where people have lived for a long time. It is a way of any life path that is walked among the Earth Mother and her children that there is always good and bad. Now, do not get this confused with some of the things that Grandfather and Two Bears have told you, because the bad has nothing to do with a lack of understanding. It is bad because it is bad."

"But, old woman," I said, "for what reason is there bad?"

"There is bad so there can be good. However, it is so much easier to see the bad because it does not require any work at all like the good does. But, since it is present in the domain of the Earth Mother, we must accept it and learn to work around it as we would do with anything that is not right for us to include in our path to understanding."

CHAPTER 24

❀

My Life Has a Meaning To It.
It Is Probably the Same As Yours.

"There are certain actions of all who walk within the Earth Mother's domain that will cause both good and bad. When our spirit leaves to return to the waiting place across the great spirit waters, then those things that we cannot take with us are left behind with her.

"This is very similar to taking a bath," the old woman said, as I could feel her look coming to the inside of me to see if I was still listening to her. "All of the things that make us dirty are left behind in the water we have been washing in. If we are successful in cleaning ourselves, then we can see the results of collecting those many things that are not a part of us remain in the bath water when we get out.

"When our spirit has finished the time that has been given to it and returns to our spirit family once again, then it is not only the shell in which we travel in that is left behind, but it is all of the emotions that are not a part of us as well.

"All of these emotions are left behind much like the leaves that fall away from the trees when the sleep season approaches. Once they fall, they do not make such a impressive sight from their numbers. However, as the wind spirit takes them to other places where they will be able to do more good for all of the Earth Mother's children, and you can see them piled up in corners of great stones, then you can see that their numbers are great and you become impressed with them.

"This is the way that the Earth Mother performs her purifying task of getting rid of all of the emotions that are left behind by those who are no longer walking a life path with her. She has given dominion over this process to all of the spirits of the land. They will search through all of the domain that is hers and as they find these emotions lying around without any owner, they will bring them to certain places where, over a period of time, they can be reduced into what they once were and be changed into a productive force to all the places where they might be needed.

"However, before this happens, and they have been reduced from a force of such intensity to one of no intensity, they can sometimes take on a life force of their own. When this happens, they will become much like a leech looking for a host in order to maintain their life.

"They do not know that they are no longer a living thing. They only remember the way that they once were and will do anything that they can do in order to maintain their existence with this domain of the Earth Mother.

"They will not listen to the spirits of the land as they tell them that their time for this form is over. In some cases, they have become such a strong emotional force that it does not seem possible that they should ever cease to exist. In fact, there have been times when their force was so intense that they have been known to take on the form of the ones that once held onto them.

"Now, you must remember that is not because they are evil that they do this, it is only because they do not understand what has happened to them. They are acting more out of fear than they are acting out of intent. With the passing of each new sun that will pass over them, they will find that they are becoming less and less than they were the day before.

"In their first effort of trying to maintain their existence within this domain that we are walking a life path through, they will attract as many other emotions of their own kind as they can find. When they become strong enough by calling other emotions that have been left behind as well, they will find a place that is the most comfortable to them and will wait in these places while calling on more and more emotions that will be able to add to their existence.

"There will always be one of those emotions who will be stronger than the others. They will be the ones who will not only call to the other emotions to join with them but will decide the direction and the actions for the rest of them to follow.

"These emotions, by themselves, have no dominion over any spirit unless that spirit willingly takes them unto themselves. However, as they become stronger, they become independent of this law that the Earth Mother has set before them. They will have the power to entice other spirits to them.

"They will realize that unless they can become attached to a spirit who is walking a life path with the Earth Mother, they will soon fade into the nothingness that they fear the most of all. So, when they have become strong, they will wait in hiding for the passing of a spirit and by fooling them into thinking they are something they are not, they will attach themselves to this spirit. They will have found a host to live in.

"The unfortunate thing about this is that if the spirit is not willing to accept them, it will cause a great illness. If this illness is not treated, then the shell in which the spirit travels in will come to a very quick end. The spirit will cross over the great spirit waters to the waiting place and the group of emotions who originally caused this to happen will be free to wait once again for another spirit to attach themselves to.

"This entire process will continue until one who knows the correct way of dispatching these emotions into the void of nothingness will come along and do such a thing.

"The reason that our people call this a bad thing is because each of the spirits who are attached by these unaccepted emotions do not ever complete their life path with the Earth Mother. Because of this, they will have to do all of this over again. So, it is all that come into contact with these groups of unwanted emotions that will suffer.

"These emotions, even though they think that they do, do not have any kind of a life path at all. They are only stopping other spirits who unknowingly come too close to them from advancing their own spirit in the life path they are walking. When this group of spirits is dispatched into the void of nothingness, no one suffers any longer and these groups of emotions will become one with the Earth Mother where they may be formed into something that is good and will benefit all who are within her domain once again."

"Is this what happened to Cheeway, old woman?" I asked, still staring at the body of my best friend laying on the floor of Grandfather's house.

"Yes, little one, this is what happened to your best friend. Now Grandfather and Two Bears are calling on the assistance of those many spirits of our families who are in the waiting place across the great spirit waters."

"What will they be able to do, old woman? They are no longer among us, and as I understand it, they do not have any more power in this domain than I do and I can feel just how helpless I am here."

"The power that they bring with them is one that will increase the power that is already within Grandfather and Two Bears. By their adding their strength to one who is still walking a life path with the Earth Mother, the one who is calling on them can be increased by more times than there are people in a village. Their increased strength and determination will allow them to over-power this group of unwanted emotions and in the end, they will be able to dispatch them in the void of nothingness."

"Will Cheeway be alright when these unwanted emotions leave him?" I asked the old woman, who still had her hand on my left shoulder.

"In time Cheeway will be find. However, the memory of what has happened to him before, during, and after this will always be with him. He will need much understanding and help from you in order to work through this event that has happened to him."

"But in time he will be the same Cheeway as he was, won't he?"

"Yes, in time he will be the same as you remembered him. You must keep in mind that the life paths that you both are walking with the Earth Mother are filled with change. Some of it will be for the good and will advance your spirit well, but other portions of these changes will not be for the good and you will have to work your way through them with the understanding that you will attain from the knowledge that you have been exposed to."

"How will we both know where to stay away from, old woman? What signs will we look for so that this will not happen to us again?"

"There will be nothing that you will be able to see with the eyes of the shell that carries you about this domain. All of the signs that will become noticeable to the both of you will only be able to be read by the eyes of the spirit. You must develop these eyes if they are ever to work for you."

"Are we only supposed to stay in our houses until this happens, old woman?" I asked, with a slight note of perturbedness in the tone of my voice.

"No, the Earth Mother does not wish to make any spirit a prisoner in her domain. The spiritual eyes that you will need have always been there but you must learn to use them. When you walk across a field, you will be warned by the spirit of places where you should not go too close to. This warning will come to you in the form of a small little voice. It will tell you, that if you are to travel in this place or another, that there is something there that is not good. It will be your job, as you learn to develop these spiritual eyes within you, to learn to listen more carefully to this voice within you. This is what I mean when I tell you that you must learn to develop your spiritual eyes that will help you to see with."

From the speaking words of the old woman, I was reminded within myself of the things that Grandfather would always tell Cheeway and myself, "You both have been given eyes, but they do not see." How appropriate this was, I was thinking, as I continued to stare at the form of Cheeway laying on Grandfather's floor.

"The song players and drum beaters are very pleasing to me, little one, are they pleasing to you as well?" the old woman asked me, with a gentle kindness in the tone of her voice.

"Yes, they are very good to hear. It makes me feel like coming to them," I answered, still keeping my eyes on the place where Cheeway was laying.

"This, if it is done correctly, is what they are supposed to do. However, when this ceremony is performed correctly, no evil will ever be able to come or stay where these sounds will travel. It would do you well to remember these sounds of this night that your people are playing. There might come a time when they will help you greatly in the times that have not yet come to you."

"Old woman," I said, putting my head back on the top of my bent knees, "you said my people, did you not mean our people?"

I waited for a few moments for a response from the old woman, but when there was none that came, I turned my head from the open doorway where Cheeway was lying and into the direction where she had been sitting. When I turned around, I did not see any trace of her at all. Even the bushes that I thought were under her were not bent over like they become when someone sits on them.

My attention was called back to the house by the opening of the screen door. Turning my head back in that direction, I saw that Grandfather was coming out of it. He had the look of many hours of work that were lying all over his face.

"Is Cheeway alright, Grandfather?" I asked, still sitting in the same position that I had begun from.

"Yes, little one, Cheeway will be alright now. We have stopped the illness that was within him."

"And the group of emotions that had attacked him, have they been dispersed back into the void of nothingness as well?"

"Yes, they are all gone now," Grandfather answered me, placing a look of confusion over his face. "How did you know of this truth when no one told you what had happened?"

"The old woman who came with Two Bears was sharing speaking words with me on this night. She told me much of what had happened to Cheeway and how you and Two Bears were helping him with the assistance of the music players and drum beaters."

"Yes, we heard you speaking to someone out here. I must admit that normally we would have sent someone out here to ask you to be quiet, but since your conversation was not bothering us in what we were attempting to perform, we decided to allow you to continue."

"Where is the old woman who was with you?" Two Bears asked, as he was walking through the screened door.

"I do not know, Two Bears. She must have gone home when I was not looking."

"How did you say that she came here?" Two Bears asked, as he continued to look into me where I sat.

"I thought that she came with you when you brought the others from the village here," I repeated once again.

"All of the others that came with me are still in the house," Two Bears said, looking in the direction of where Grandfather was standing.

"Where was she during this conversation, little one?" Grandfather asked me.

"Here," I said, pointing to the large stone that was behind me. "She was sitting here and telling me of all the things that were going on inside of the house."

Keeping my eyes on Grandfather and Two Bears, I could see that their faces went completely void of expression and were being lit by a blue glowing light that seemed to be coming from behind me now.

I turned my head to see where it was coming from. When I did, I saw that there was a small circle of light that had formed just above the large stone that was behind me. As the light became brighter, it began to circle all three of us then it went into the house where Cheeway and the others of our village were.

As the glowing circle of light went into the house, we all followed it with our eyes and could see that it placed itself just above where Cheeway was laying on the floor. There was a glowing that seemed to surround Cheeway from the light above him. Then, as quickly as it had begun, it disappeared and left the sight of all who had seen it.

There was no noise within the house, there was only silence but that was broken by Grandfather's voice when he said, "You say that you only called her Old Woman?"

"Yes, Grandfather," I said, having gotten out of my sitting position and into a standing one.

"Our people know of this one. We call her She Who Comes To Comfort and Heal."

Looking at me with a very good look on his face he continued: "You should feel very honored that one such as her had come to give you comfort on this night, little one. It has not been many who have ever been able to share speaking words with her. They have only felt her and the blessings that she has brought upon our people. Before you go off with the dream spirits on this night, you must tell her how much you enjoyed sharing speaking words with her so she will know that you will remember."

"I will do this, Grandfather," I said, as I continued to look at the position where Cheeway was lying. I could see that he was beginning to move once again. In a very short time, I saw that he was being helped to his feet by those who had come with Two Bears.

Seeing that Cheeway was going to be alright, I turned my head from the house and into the small dirt path that ran by Grandfather's house. I could hear the wind spirit playing with the leaves that had been gathered in some of the corners of the surrounding buildings. For the first time in what felt like a long time, I could feel that there was still the peace of the Earth Mother's left that I could feel.

I was getting very tired and had decided to go into the house to lay down and travel with the dream spirits for another night. However, I did not forget what Grandfather had told me to do and as I laid down on one of the blankets that had been spread out in the corner of one of the rooms, I closed my eyes and said my gratitude to the old woman.

Just as I was beginning to feel the dream spirit lift me away for the night, I heard the old woman's voice come to me once again: "For those who can remember, there is no need to repeat."

PART IX

❀

A PLACE OF REMEMBERING

CHAPTER 25

❀

Returning

It had been several months since Cheeway accidentally walked into the place of strong emotions and had become very ill. We had shared our speaking words with each other many times over this time and I was finally getting the impression that all that had happened to him that day was almost finished having any kind of effect on him.

When Cheeway had asked me if I would like to go with him to one of the old villages on the land of the mesa, I knew that he was alright now and was once again himself. I told him that I would like to go with him and soon we were getting things ready for our trip to this place.

The following morning, as I was sitting on the front porch of my parents' house, I heard the familiar sound of a truck coming down the dirt path that led to our house. Looking down the street, I could see that it was Grandfather's truck and seated with him in the cab was Cheeway.

I was very surprised to see Grandfather bringing Cheeway with him because I had not planned on him coming with us on this day.

Finally, the truck pulled into our driveway as I motioned it in from the front porch. I could see that both Grandfather and Cheeway had very large smiles on their faces.

Coming to a complete stop in the drive, I walked over to the truck and gave them our customary greetings.

"Well, little one, I see that you are all packed and ready to go," Grandfather said, still sitting behind the wheel of the truck.

"Yes, I am, Grandfather," I responded to him, but looking a little confused by this unexpected turn of events. "Will you be coming with us on this morning?"

"Yes, I thought that it would be a very good idea for me to take you both to a place where you might really be able to find something. Do you mind this change of plans?" Grandfather asked, as he was looking deep within me for the answer that I would finally give to him.

"No, I do not mind. Each time that you take Cheeway and me to a place, we are able to learn great things because of the speaking words that you share with us," I said, still holding my sack of provisions.

"Very well then, why don't you get into the truck with us and we will get started. I have a very good place in mind that I want to take the both of you to but in order to see all that I want to show you, we will need much of this day that we are in."

Getting into the truck, I could tell by the look that was on Cheeway's face that he did not have any idea of the place we were going to either. We both knew Grandfather well enough to know better than to ask him anything that he was not willing to tell us. So sitting down in the truck, we began backing out of the driveway and heading down the dirt street that ran in front of my parents' house.

We had been traveling for about an hour when Grandfather stopped his truck at a place on the mesa. He announced to the both of us that we were here and that we should go to the back of the truck and get out those provisions that we had brought with us.

I looked over at Cheeway's face and was surprised to see that the look told me that this place was not a new one to him. In fact, the look that was on the his face told me that he was wishing that he was not here at all.

Grandfather saw this look come over Cheeway's face and I knew that he was able to see the same thing as I did. When I looked over to where Grandfather was standing, I could see that there were many thoughts that were running through his mind. I knew that he was searching for the correct speaking words to share with both Cheeway and myself.

"Grandfather, why have you brought me here?" Cheeway asked, with a trembling sound in his voice.

"Because it is for the best that you return to this place before the passing of another season," Grandfather said, as he continued to look at Cheeway.

There was a profound silence in the air after these speaking words had been shared by Grandfather and Cheeway. Not wanting to interfere with their self-proclaimed silence, I quietly moved to the back of the truck and took out all of the provisions that we had brought with us for this trip.

As I unloaded the back of the truck, I could feel the uneasiness in the silence that was all around me and putting the provisions that we had brought with us in the front of the truck, I decided to ask Grandfather what this was all about.

"Grandfather," I said, setting down the last of the bundles that we had brought with us, "why is Cheeway so concerned with this place that you have brought us both to?"

"It is because this is the place where he accidentally walked into the group of emotions that had made him very ill before," Grandfather said, searching in one of his pockets for something.

"Is this why Cheeway is frightened of this place?" I asked, standing very close to where Cheeway was.

"Yes, little one," Grandfather answered. "Here is where Cheeway must learn to face his fears if he is ever going to be able to learn from them. This is only one of the reasons why I have brought you both here though. The other reason is that there is another thing that I wish to share with the both of you in this place. But I will not be able to do this unless Cheeway learns to master himself from the experience that he went through before."

"Does this place still frighten you, Cheeway?" I asked, putting my right hand on his left shoulder.

"Yes, this place still has a great power over me even now," Cheeway said, staring out into the direction where the old village was.

"Do you know that it is better to face an enemy than it is to try to hide from him?" I asked.

"That is the only reason that I am not running away from this place right now," Cheeway said, in return to my speaking words.

"It is time for us to begin our journey," Grandfather said, as he picked up one of the sacks that we had brought our provisions in. "Come now, we still have a ways to go before we can confront this thing that Cheeway must do."

Finishing his speaking words to us, Grandfather started off in the direction of the old village. I looked at Cheeway and I could tell that he was battling many things that were within himself. I was hoping that the warrior that was within him would be strong enough for him to win this battle. I knew that if it was, then there would be great blessings on him, and his spirit would be able to advance even more because of this.

I began following Grandfather as he was walking away from the truck, and within a few moments, I was very relieved to hear the sounds of Cheeway's footsteps following behind us. I knew, as Grandfather did, that Cheeway would have to do most of this on his own. No matter how much I wanted to help him, there was not much that I could do, other than be there for him on this test that he was going through.

In silence, we walked for about one half hour, and finally reaching the place where Grandfather wanted to bring us to, he sat down his sack of provisions and looked at the both of us who were still coming to the place where he was.

"Come now," came his voice to us. "We are here now and the worst is over for you, Cheeway, because you have made this journey. Now comes the easy part for you as you will learn to close another chapter in the life path that you are walking with the Earth Mother."

I could see that Cheeway was breathing very hard now and I knew that it could not be from the distance that we had traveled. There was only one other reason that I could think of for his breathing to be so hard and that was that he was fighting very hard within himself. He was fighting his feelings with his warrior spirit. I knew that he was winning this battle.

I looked back to the position where Cheeway was walking from and smiled at him. I knew that he appreciated this because it told him that we all knew what he was going through and that we were with him.

Smiling back at both of us, Cheeway picked up his step and continued to the place where we were waiting for him. Reaching this position, Cheeway laid his sack of provisions down on the ground next to ours and sat down.

"I am very tired, Grandfather," Cheeway said, wiping the sweat off from the top of his head. "Do you think that we could rest now…just for a short while?"

"Just for awhile, Cheeway," Grandfather said. "You must keep in mind that you are almost finished with this battle and so far, you have been winning. Now is not the time to stop it though."

Cheeway nodded his head in an up and down manner to tell him that he understood what he had told him and that he agreed with it. We rested for a few minutes then we got back up and continued our journey back into the old village where Cheeway had his encounter.

As we were walking into the old village, I could not ignore my feelings any longer and I knew that I would have to share speaking words with Grandfather.

I waited for a time when Cheeway was walking far enough behind us so that he would not be able to over hear what I had to say.

"Grandfather," I said, walking very close to him now.

"Yes, little one, what is it that troubles you so on this fine day?"

"It is this thing that you are doing with Cheeway. It worries me that he is being so pained by this experience."

"Tell me, little one, why does it bother you so much?" Grandfather replied, to the speaking words that I had shared with him.

I could tell by the tone of his voice that he was going to answer my question for me but he was also going to make me think for it.

"Why is it wise for us to bring Cheeway back to this place where all of his troubles have begun? Would it not be better to simply let him forget them and all of the hurt and pain that they brought to him?"

"Let me answer your question with another question, little one. If you saw that Cheeway was cut and his arm was bleeding, would you not try to stop it from bleeding?"

"Why, yes, Grandfather, I would do this for him."

"Now then, once you have stopped the arm from bleeding, would you just pretend that there was nothing else wrong with it?"

"No, Grandfather, I would not fool myself in thinking that just because the bleeding has stopped."

"Well, then, what would you do?" Grandfather asked me, as he purposely slowed down our pace just to the point that Cheeway would be able to catch up with us.

"Well, I would get him to a place where they would make sure that all things were healed on his arm and anything else that might have suffered during this bleeding."

"And what makes you think that anything else could have suffered by his arm bleeding. After all, it was only the arm that was cut."

"You have told us often that from one place of injury many others could be affected by it. I would believe that if the body had lost too much blood that it would make him very weak and he would perhaps need more blood to replace that which he had lost."

"And if it was your blood that was needed, little one, would you give your blood to Cheeway so that he would feel better?"

"Yes, I would do this for Cheeway because he is my brother in the life path that we are walking with the Earth Mother."

"Now, you agree that you would do this for him but you also say that you would need the advice of one who is more experienced than you to make the determination as to whether Cheeway would need this or not?"

"Yes, I would not be able to tell because I have not had enough experience in such things."

"And you would take Cheeway to another with more experience than you for this advice?"

"Yes, Grandfather, as you have always told us, the true measure of caring for another comes not from the eyes but from the heart. This would be my reason for taking Cheeway to another of greater experience than I would have at this time."

"Well, little one, this is exactly what we are doing for Cheeway on this day and back at the same village ruins that we are in."

"You mean that the pain and suffering that Cheeway has gone through could have more meaning than what we have been able to see? But Cheeway and I have been playing for many days now and he seems to be very much himself. What makes you think that there is still something wrong with him?"

"Little one," Grandfather replied, "what makes you think that there is not something wrong with him?"

I could not argue with any of the speaking words that he had shared with me. As usual, the way that Grandfather had answered my questions to him were in a way that allowed me to answer them for myself from the limited amounts of experience that I had been able to gather in the seasons of my own life path that I knew.

What Grandfather had shared with me somehow told me that his love was one that was far beyond any that either Cheeway or I had the ability to understand. However, I wanted to hear from his speaking words that this was a love that I did not understand.

"Grandfather," I said, as I continued walking close to him in the direction of the old village of ruins, "is the reason that you are doing this for Cheeway because you love him?"

Grandfather looked down at me but did not stop his walking pace. I could see by the look that was in his eyes that this question that I had put to him was a very deep one, one that was far deeper than I may have realized at that time.

"Yes, little one, it is from love for Cheeway that I am doing this. I am very pleased that you were able to see this. I can know from this day on that you will meet that one who has been placed in this domain for you."

"Grandfather?' I said, still looking up at him.

"Yes?"

"Is this love more than I can understand at this time in my life path?" I asked, not knowing what the answer to me would be.

"There is no such thing as being in a place where you cannot understand anything, little one. The truth of the matter is that many times we are in a place where we will not accept that which is being given to us."

"Am I able to accept this kind of love that you are giving to Cheeway, Grandfather?"

"What do you think, little one?"

As he finished these speaking words to me, he turned his head as he once again slowed down his pace to make sure that Cheeway was behind us...close enough so that he would be able to hear these speaking words that we were sharing if he was ready to accept them.

"I think that I am ready to accept them, Grandfather," I said, as I too looked behind me to see where Cheeway was.

When I turned my head to look at Cheeway, I was very surprised to see that his face was no longer a tormented one but it was one that was filled with the look of curiosity once again. I knew that because Cheeway had been able to hear some of the speaking words that we were sharing. He was gaining strength from them and it was beginning to show on him. He was no longer walking as if he had the weight of the entire mesa over him. He was beginning to walk with the lightness of feet that I had always known him to have.

"Little one," Grandfather said to me, "are you ready to hear another truth before I tell you the one that you have asked?"

"Yes," I said, not knowing what this addition to our speaking words would bring.

"It is not you who is asking these questions, but it is your spirit who is reaching out to Cheeway through me. It is your spirit who is guiding my speaking words to both you and Cheeway and it is good."

As I looked up at Grandfather and saw the large smile that he held over his face, I could not help myself at first but to feel very proud because this was the first time in my life on the mesa with him that he had ever paid me such a great compliment. However, after this self admiration wore off, I came back into myself and the things that I wanted to find out from his wisdom, and this new kind of love that we were going to hear about.

CHAPTER 26

The Spirit of Caring

"You see, little one," Grandfather began his speaking words to me, "in the beginning, there is only the kind of love that you are able to feel from your mother and father. This kind of love is a totally giving love, but it is not a teaching love.

"The giving love that a parent gives to the child is one that is filled with the protection that is instinctive in all those who walk a life path with her. While this love gives us great pleasure and security, it does not give us the learning that we will need to develop our spirits.

"However, this love comes to all who begin their life path because there is a great need for protection. As young children, we do not have the ability of protecting ourselves from many things that will confront us in these early seasons of our life path. However, if this early love is left to the child long after they are children, then it become a very bad thing because that spirit will not grow into the beautiful being that they were meant to be."

"It is almost like being always young, isn't it?" I asked, making sure that we were not traveling too fast for Cheeway who was still behind us.

"Yes, in a way you are correct, little one. It is almost like being always young. But think of it in this way. If you and Cheeway were not ever to advance your spirits, then what you would find in your life would not help you to find what I have been able to learn.

"Now, when both of you come to me, you come to me with many things. One of those things that you often bring me is concern over something that is bothering you. You come to me expecting me to help you to understand or work your way through these things. Is this not correct?"

I did not want to interrupt his speaking words that he was sharing with us so I simply nodded my head in an up and down manner so that he would be able to see that I was agreeing with him.

"Well then, what would happen if I were to have stayed only with the first love that I knew...the one that my parents gave to me? You see, I would not have gained my wisdom in this life path that I am walking, but I would have only stayed as mature and as wise as one of your seasons.

"If I had stayed with this giving and very secure love that I knew as a young child, when you would come to me, all that I would be able to share with you would be the things that you already know. I do not believe that either of you would find this to be a great help in understanding all of the things that have happened to both of you in this life path you are walking with the Earth Mother."

"Well, Grandfather," I said, "where does this wisdom of yours that we continually seek come from?"

"It comes from the journey to the more advanced state of love that I am speaking to you about on this day. Without having traveled through this journey and having learned from it, I would not have been capable of seeing the necessity of giving Cheeway the assistance so that he might be able to help himself as we are doing on this day and in this old village of ruins that we are in.

"What I have learned from this way of loving is that it is not always the words or actions of another that will ask one who is very close to them for help. Most of the time, it is the spirit's voice that will come to you and will ask you for the correct type of help that it needs. This voice will call to you from the inside and unless you have ears that come from the spirit within you, you will not ever know the correct thing to do for one whom you care deeply for.

"It is very important to understand this, little one. This will be the only way that you will be capable of truly giving the kind of love that another needs in the life path that they are walking.

"You see, if I could not hear the spirit of Cheeway calling to me for the kind of help that he truly needed, then I would be only capable of giving to him those things that my parents gave to me when I was young. And that would be to speak softly to him and to periodically caress the top of his head and tell him that all things will be alright because I am here.

"However, this would not benefit Cheeway at all. It would be very unfair to him and to all those who were around him because nothing would have been settled…and nothing would have been learned…and nothing would have been worked through. Because of this, there would be no understanding accomplished and the spirit would not advance any further than it was when his troubles had began.

"When you will learn to listen to the call of the spirit, you will understand what it is that it needs. And because of the love that you will have for this other person, you will know the necessity of doing those things that are correct for this spirit to continue with its learning and understanding. After all, we must keep in the front of our minds that this is what we have come to the Earth Mother for.

"Now, what you see from the point of your understanding and what I can see from my point of understanding are very different. They are different because I have traveled on this journey to learn a more understanding love than you have at this point in your life path.

"I realize that from the prospective that you are at, that you only see what I am doing on this day is hurting Cheeway. I also see that Cheeway is hurting, but I also understand what he needs to stop his hurting and this is what I am doing.

"From the point that you are at, you see only the hurting that he is going through because you have not learned enough to see otherwise. I see what will become of Cheeway if he does not perform those things that he must perform. Because of the love that I have for him, I have chosen to answer his spirit's call to me so that he will be able to continue with the advancement of his spirit.

"This then is only one of the portions of a mature love for another. It is knowing that while something may give them a little pain today, that the benefits that it will bring to them in the seasons that are ahead of them will be great. It is loving them enough to walk through their pain with them and helping them to see all those things that they must learn in order to arrive at the place where they should be in tomorrow."

When Grandfather had finished his speaking words to me, we continued our walk into the direction of the old village ruins in silence. I knew that his speaking words held great meaning to me, and I also knew that since Cheeway had been so close to both of us during this sharing, that he too would find great meaning in them.

As unnoticeable as possible, I turned my head so that I could catch a glimpse of Cheeway out of the corner of one of my eyes. When he came into my view, I was very relieved to see that he had placed a small smile over his face. He was no longer only looking down on the ground beneath him, but he was now looking at Grandfather with a look of better understanding in his eyes.

"Grandfather," came the speaking words from Cheeway, "I am ready now to do this thing that I must do."

Grandfather had stopped his forward motion and turned to look at Cheeway.

"This is very good, Cheeway," Grandfather answered him, standing in a position that allowed him to look directly at him. "Do you feel a need to do something that will allow you to feel the freedom of what is still traveling within you?"

"Yes, Grandfather," Cheeway said, "I still feel that something is within me but I did not want to say anything because I was scared of it."

Cheeway's speaking words surprised me because I was not even aware that there was anything else that was bothering him from that experience that he had had on this land.

"Well then, Cheeway, would you like to know what it is that you should do?" Grandfather said to him.

"Yes, I would walk in your words of wisdom," came the reply from Cheeway.

"Very good then, Cheeway," Grandfather said, with a large smile on the front of his face. "Go to the place where the group of emotions first attached themselves to you and sit. Once you have sat in this place where they once waited, think of only the love that you understand and have felt from the Earth Mother. By doing this, you will allow a healing to take place over this land where there was once only bad things on it. Then the spirits of the land will return this favor you do for them with a healing that they will place over you."

Hearing his speaking words to him, Cheeway walked off and into the place where he first encountered this group of emotions and he sat down and closed his eyes. I could tell from the look that was over his face that he was not comfortable with this at all, but because of the faith that he held in all that Grandfather had shared with him, he did what was asked of him.

We had been watching Cheeway as he was sitting on this land for about twenty minutes. Out of nowhere, Cheeway began to sing a spirit caller's song. It was not one that I could ever remember hearing before and from the look that was over Grandfather's face, it was not one that he had heard either. However, we both knew that this was an act of the spirit that lived within Cheeway and we sat patiently and listened to the singing words that he was sharing with us.

As we sat and listened to the spirit song that Cheeway was singing, I could tell that some of the words that were clear to me were about giving thanks to the spirits of the land for allowing him the opportunity of being able to return to this place and complete a needed healing. He was also singing of the joy and happiness that he had found in being able to confront his fears with his warrior spirit and how much better he felt in being able to do such a thing.

This was becoming confusing to me because I knew of all of the work that Grandfather had made in order to get Cheeway out to this place where he would be able to do such a thing. I knew that Cheeway was not very happy about it and would have run away from this place if it had not been for Grandfather repeatedly encouraging him to continue. Now, it seemed to me that Cheeway was in a place where he was saying that this was what he wanted to do all the time and this was very confusing to me.

"Grandfather?" I said, as I was sitting next to him on a soft piece of the land we were on.

"Yes, little one," Grandfather replied to me, "what is it?"

"I am confused by Cheeway's singing words. He makes it seem as though this was what he had wanted to do to all along. However, I know better because I saw the look that came over his face from the time that the truck brought us to this place and it was not a look of wanting to do this at all."

"You must remember, little one, that the one who you know as Cheeway in this life path that you are walking with is not the one who you are hearing singing such a great spirit song. The Cheeway that you know does not even know that such a spirit song exists.

"The Cheeway you are hearing sing such a spirit song is his spirit. Remember when I told you that it was his spirit that I was listening to? It was his spirit that had asked me to make such an opportunity available to him so that he would be able to complete his healing process. Well, the song that you are hearing now should be proof to you that I was correct. Because Cheeway is not fully in touch with his spirit yet, just as you are not, I must listen carefully to each of your spirits when they seek out my assistance in their times of need. Let this be a great lesson to you in the difference of being able to hear from the view of a more advanced love...one that is learned through the path that I have traveled in this life path that I am on. Let this serve to guide you as well because of the greater ways that you may be able to give your caring to those who you will become close to in the life path that you are walking with the Earth Mother.

Remember, that it is by this kind of a love for others that you will grow in understanding and this will cause your spirit to advance greatly."

"Grandfather," I asked once again, as I looked up to him, "why was it not possible for Cheeway's spirit to tell him to ask for help from you through himself instead of making you do such great work?"

"This has happened to Cheeway as it happens to all who are walking a life path with the Earth Mother. For Cheeway, he was going through his changes and the event that had happened to him on this land accentuated this change for him. Now, when change comes to any of us, it causes us great pain in the bodies that are used by our spirits to travel in. These bodies value things that do not change and when they are exposed to things that will cause this thing called change, they will react in very predictable ways.

"However, these ways that the body reacts will cause any of the communication that was ever there with the spirit that lives within to stop. This is what had happened to Cheeway. The spirit was not able to speak to him because his body was so busy trying to adjust to the changes that were taking place within him. That was using up all of his mind that was available to him.

"Does this happen to you as well, Grandfather?" I asked.

"Sometimes, it does, little one. When it does, I too must seek out the assistance of those who are close to me. However, one of the lessons that we will try to learn and understand is how to make the spirit strong enough within us that it will have the power to overcome these types of things when they happen. This is a very important thing that we have all set out before us in all of the life paths that are being walked with the Earth Mother, her children, and the spirits of the land.

"Each time that we make another effort, and are successful in overcoming this situation, it not only delights our own spirits, but all within the domain of the Earth Mother will be delighted as well. They know another spirit who has come to them is progressing.

"Perhaps now would be a good time to share this wisdom with you. I believe that the need for this will come to all of us again, and when it does, I know that Cheeway will benefit from this sharing as well."

CHAPTER 27

꧁

The Three Spirits of Change

"In all of the changes that will come to us in our life path, there are three spirits who will be attached to them. First, there will be the spirit of denial. This spirit will try to convince you that the change before you does not really matter and, if you will just ignore it, then all of the feelings of badness will leave and you will not have to worry about it any more. However, as it is with all things in the domain of the Earth Mother's that we walk through, you will be given a choice. You will be allowed to choose to accept the spirit of denial. If you do this, there will be no advancement or understanding gained from this valuable gift of change that is being offered to you. Or you will accept the challenge of the change that is confronting you and begin to advance to the next spirit that will be waiting.

"This next spirit that will be waiting for you is the spirit of anger. This spirit of anger will tell you that this change that has come to you is not now, nor has it ever been, meant for you. It is only a bothersome thing that is getting in the way of your happiness and good feelings in the life path you is walking. The spirit of anger tells you that you are a very strong being and that there is nothing that can stand in your way that you will not be able to knock down and then walk over. This spirit tells you that all the things that are available to you are your right. To those things that stop you from finding the peace and happiness that you once had is not your friend and you should destroy it. Once again, you will have a choice of either accepting this spirit's advice to you or trying to work through this second part of the change within you. Once again, I want you to remember that if you accept and listen to this spirit of anger and follow his advice, then there will be no advancement of your spirit because there has been nothing that has been learned or understood. Now, if you choose to work through this second part of the change that has come to you, you will be greeted by the third spirit of change.

"This third and final spirit of change is the spirit of acceptance. It is here that you will come to understand the value of being able to work through all changes that will come to you. It is from this spirit that you will come to know and understand that all change that will come to you is to be considered as a gift. This spirit will tell you just how important these things are to you. This spirit of acceptance tells you that all of the things that you and your spirit have been willing to work their way through have allowed you to grow even more than you had before this change had come to you. This spirit, once it has shown to you all of the benefits and the different ways that your spirit will be able to advance, will give you a peace and calmness that will allow your spirit to come for you to see it. It is at this time, when your body and spirit can see each other and a new level of understanding takes place. The spirit will grow in its strength and the body will see the value of the spirit more. Remember, each time that you are successful in working through all change that will come to you, your spirit will continue to get stronger and your body will see this value of the spirit that lives within you. It will not resist the spirit as much as it did before you encountered the change that you have just worked through.

"This is what Cheeway has just accomplished. This is what his spirit is so happy about being able to do. However, because of short number of seasons with the Earth Mother, he still requires the help of one such as I. In time, both of you will have been given the opportunity of advancing your spirits sufficiently so that you will be able to do such things without my assistance. When this happens, you will be able to see that it is good."

CHAPTER 28

❀

Giving Thanks

With his speaking words completed to me, he turned his head and once again observed all of the things that Cheeway was doing. I, too, turned my head to observe Cheeway, and as I did, I could see that there was already a new kind of growing that was taking place within him.

Finishing his spirit caller's song, Cheeway continued to sit in silence. As we continued to watch him, we could see that a very pleasant peace was coming into him. It was at this point that I knew that all of the things that Grandfather had shared with me on our way out to this place held great truth in them. Grandfather was right…it was good.

Having finished his spirit song, Cheeway opened his eyes and began looking around himself for something. His eyes seemed to fall on a small stone that was lying next to him. Bending his back and stretching out his arm, he picked up this small stone with one of his hands.

Standing up, he turned around to look at the mark that his body had left in the soft dirt that was on this land. Once he found where he had been sitting on this ground, he placed the small stone in the middle of the position then walked off from it and did not look back.

"Why did Cheeway do this thing?" I asked Grandfather, still sitting in the same place that we had begun from.

"This is Cheeway's way of giving thanks to the spirits of the land and giving himself a small marker of where an event has taken place that has allowed a spirit to grow with the Earth Mother. This is the mark that the spirit makes when it has overcome a great obstacle in the life path that it is walking."

"Is Cheeway going to be Cheeway now, or will we still be speaking to his spirit that lives within him?"

"By the time that Cheeway comes to us, he will be himself once again. You will know him once again as the one who you have been traveling through this life path with."

When Cheeway finally reached our positions, we had stood up and exchanged greetings once again. I could see that Cheeway was the one who I remembered. This was a very good feeling for me. I could tell that he had come back to us completely and I was very glad that all that we had gone through with him was done. I was very happy now and I could also feel the peace and the freedom that Cheeway was feeling. However, there was a new kind of growth and strength of his spirit that I was feeling from him. I knew that this was a good sign.

As we continued with our walk through this village of ruins, I could feel that from the strength that was now a part of Cheeway's spirit. It would allow my own spirit to grow just because we were close to one another. And as we continued to share our speaking words, I could hear that this strength would not leave Cheeway. It would stay with him and allow his spirit to advance in the life path that it was on.

PART X

A WHISPER THROUGH TIME

CHAPTER 29

❀

Entry Way

We were continuing our walk through this village of ruins. Cheeway and I had been so busy sharing speaking words with each other that I had completely forgotten that Grandfather told us both that there were two reasons that he wanted to bring us to this place. That is, until he stopped in his walking path and reminded us once again that we were in the place where he wanted us to be.

"We are here, little ones," came the speaking words to us, as we looked up and to the place where he was standing.

"Where are we, Grandfather?" I asked, with a tone of confusion in the sound of my own voice.

"We are at the second place I told you both about. Do you not remember?" Grandfather asked both of us, with a look in his eyes that told us that he was not at all pleased with our short memories.

"I will be very surprised one day when the both of you will be able to remember at least some of the things that I share with you," Grandfather continued, "Yes, I will be very surprised indeed."

Finishing his speaking words to us, he turned and walked to a place that was on the wall of the great stone in front of us. As we followed him, we could see that he was walking to an opening that had not been visible to us before. He paused and turned to both of us once again.

"Reach into one of the sacks that we have brought with us and get a small piece of food for me, will you?" Grandfather asked of us, as he stood in the front of the opening.

"What would you like to eat, Grandfather?" I asked, holding the opening of my bag near my right hand.

"It is not for me that I am asking. It is for the one who comes here often to see what he has left for us. It would not be considered polite if we were to see his work and not leave something for him to eat."

Reaching into my sack, I looked at Cheeway. I could see by the look that was on his face that he was just as confused as I was about this. However, in all of the times that we have heard Grandfather's speaking words to us, there was not ever a time when the truth that they held within them was not shown to us over the time that we would spend with him.

I had pulled out a roll of fresh baked bread that we had brought with us, and handing it to Grandfather, I asked him why it was so important that we leave something at the opening of the cave.

"If you had walked a complete life path searching for an answer that you could not find, then in the final season of the time that was left to you, you decided to leave a spirit painting for others who might have the same kinds of problems that you had, would it not be fair to request that some kind of a payment be left for you?" Grandfather told us, as he placed the loaf of bread on a small ledge that had been chiseled out of the rock opening to the cave.

"Grandfather," I said, still looking at him place the bread into the small opening, "how will this person eat our bread if you squash it so tightly into the opening of this cave?"

"It is for him to see that it is there. He is no longer capable of eating the food that gives us nourishment," came his reply.

Cheeway and I did not understand at all what he was doing. We could only stand in the positions that we were in and watch him place the large loaf of bread into a very small hole that was in the rock.

Finishing this task, Grandfather turned around to look at us both and said, "I suppose that now would be a good time to explain to each of you what it is that I am doing.

"Have a seat on the outside of the cave here where the ground is still soft and I will explain to you some of the past events that have taken place on this place where we are."

CHAPTER 30

❀

The Song Legend of Stands Alone

Grandfather made a motion to the both of us that we should have a seat. As he was making his motion to both of us, he made a place for himself as well in the soft dirt that was beneath us.

"You both remember how I told you that it is not uncommon to find bad residing next to the good, don't you?" he began his speaking words to the both of us.

"Yes, Grandfather," we both said in unison. "We remember these speaking words that you shared with us before."

"Well, in this place, there was once a great village. There was a place which is now inside of the cave we are about to go into that is very good. This goodness comes from one of our people who lived many generations ago. It is what he has left to us, with the help of many of the spirits of the land, that helps us to remember things that are of truth and importance in the life path we are on.

"His name was Stands Alone and he lived among our people when we had not been in these lands of the Earth Mother's for many generations. Many of our people of that time still remembered the song legend of how the fire bird brought our people from a land where there was much misery and hate for them through the tunnels that run beneath the Earth Mother and into the valley of healing where our people rested before they were allowed to roam freely once again in this domain.

"It was a time when there were many great deeds and quests that were being performed by our people. When they would succeed, there would be great feasts for them in their honor."

Grandfather paused for a moment and we could tell that he was putting his thoughts together so that these speaking words that he was sharing with both of us would not be confused by other events.

"As I have said, his name was Stands Alone. He was of a large family in this village and he had, as our song legends tell it, six brothers and five sisters. Their family was the largest of the entire village and everything that they would do would be known by all that were around them.

"The village was the main source for all that they had, though, because his father did not hunt or work and his mother was too tired from bringing in so many children. Because of this, all of the children who lived within this family knew that were it not for the goodness of the rest of the village, that they would not have the means to provide for themselves.

"There were always many cruel words that were spoken to this family by the children of the village. Having so many of these cruel words aimed at him, Stands Alone felt very bad about being brought into a family such as the one that he had.

"He did not ever let any opportunity go by to think how much better off he would be if he had no family at all.

Whenever he would think of this, he would walk into the surrounding hills and stay for weeks at a time. No one would ever know where he would go on these times, but whenever he would come back to the village, he would be filled with many great deeds that he had performed.

"In the beginning, many of the children of the village believed him, but with the passing of additional seasons in all of their life paths, they came to know that those things that Stands Alone said that he had accomplished could just not be true.

"It was one of those times when he had decided to spend another couple of weeks away from the village that it finally happened. When Stands Alone went off and into the surrounding hills, several of the young men followed him. They were very careful though, so that their presence would not be known by Stands Alone. They wanted to see what it was that he did when he disappeared from their village.

"They followed Stands Alone for most of that day before he had finally come to rest in a valley that he had found. As they watched him, and what he was doing, they found out that all that he had told them was not entirely lies. Those things that Stands Alone said that he had accomplished in fact he had done…only it was with the small world that he had built for himself from sticks and mud that represented all of the quests that he said that he had done.

"When the young men of the village saw what he was doing, they decided to go back to the village and tell the others what they had found. They left very quietly so that Stands Alone would not hear them as they left. Some of them began to laugh, while others of them were marking their trail to this place where Stands Alone had created his own world to live in.

"It was about two weeks later when Stands Alone walked into the village with his new tales of quests that he had performed. Just as he was about to finish with the first of his stories, one of the young men of the village came forward and explained what they had seen Stands Alone doing when he left the village and went to his special place in the hills.

"All those who were gathered around him did not get angry like the young men of the village thought that they would, but they all began to laugh at Stands Alone. However, to Stands Alone, this was much worse than anything that they could have ever done. When he saw all of those who were gathered around him laughing, he turned away from them and ran out of the village and into the plains that were next to them.

"Some of the villagers said that they saw tears coming out of his face as he ran past them. It was because of this incident that a young girl of the village decided that this was too cruel of a fate for even one such as Stands Alone. She decided to follow after him to share speaking words with him."

CHAPTER 31

❀

Spirit of Wind Song

"Her name was Wind Song and she had about seven seasons less to her life path than Stands Alone did. She was of a good spirit and her heart was telling her that someone needed to share speaking words with Stands Alone because she knew something of the pain that he was feeling. She had seen this kind of a pain on her older sister when she found that she could not give her husband any children. She remembered hearing her sister cry alone at night in her lodging because the other young women of the village would torment her by bringing their children close to her and this would give her great pain.

"So Wind Song knew what some of the pain that Stands Alone was going through when his actions were found out by the young men of the village.

"When she finally came to the place where Stands Alone was sitting, she could see that his heart was filled with a heaviness. She could tell this because of the way that he was sitting on the edge of one of the great rocks that were on this land of theirs.

"'Stands Alone!' Wind Song cried out.

"Stands Alone turned his head in the direction of her voice and saw that she was coming to him. He had decided that it would not be good to wait for her to come to him and began to run off and away from her.

"'Stands Alone!' Wind Song cried out once again. 'Why do you run away from me? I have only come to you so that we might share speaking words that will make you feel better.'

"Stands Alone, hearing her voice, stopped his running and turned around to wait for Wind Song to come to him.

"'Why did you run from me, Stands Alone?' Wind Song asked.

"'I do not need any more laughing at me on this day,' came the reply of Stands Alone.

"'I did not come to laugh at you for what you have done. Even though I do not agree with what you have done, I am prepared to listen to your speaking words which give your reasons why you would do such a thing,' Wind Song said.

"'You could not know my reasons for doing such a thing,' Stands Alone told Wind Song. 'You have a family that has a place in the village. You have things that are yours. You can walk through our people with your head held up and your basket full of things that are yours to give or to keep. I cannot do such things.

"'I have a family that does nothing. I do not have anything at all in my basket that is mine. I do not have a family that has any place in the village where we live. I can only look at the ground where I am walking as I pass by any of the people who are there.

"'So,' Stands Alone asked, 'how is it that someone like you can understand anything of this at all?'

"'I understand this, Stands Alone,' Wind Song said, putting her hands over her hips. 'I understand that you and your family are two separate persons. The things that your family does, you have no control over, but the things that you do you can control. You must learn that you are the only one who can accept responsibility for what will happen to you.

"'Now,' Wind Song continued, 'if you wish to change things in the way that others in the village see you, then you must stop feeling so very sorry for yourself. You must make something out of yourself so that you will be able to walk among the others of our village with your head held straight and your basket filled with the things that are yours to give or to keep. In this way, Stands Alone, you will be able to become that which you have only been pretending to be.

"'It will not be until you have decided to stop feeling sorry for yourself, and hiding from the true things in your life path, that things will begin to change for you. And those things will not come to you unless you are willing to work for them very hard.'

"'You care for me, Wind Song?' Stands Alone asked her.

"'Yes, Stands Alone, I care for you,' Wind Song replied to him. 'However, I only care for you in the way that I see you. Not the one who ran out of our village on this day. I care for the you that is yet to be. I care for the you that is willing to work very hard so that he may stand straight and say, look…all that I have is mine because I have worked for it.'

"'You will see, Wind Song. I will be this person who you will be able to care for.'

"Having shared these speaking words with each other, they both walked back to the village where there were others of the young men waiting for their return.

"When these young men saw that Wind Song was returning to the village with Stands Alone, they became very angry and decided that it was time for Stands Alone to leave. They ran up to him and hit him with many things. Finally, as Stands Alone was laying of the ground, they stood over him and told him that there was no need for him to be in this village any longer.

"Stands Alone knew that they were right. If he were to become the one who Wind Song wanted him to be, then he would have to become this new person in another village where his past would not be known. However, as he stood up, he held out a closed fist to all of those young men who were standing before him and told them that he would come back one day. When he did, there would not be any room for them in this village that they were now living in.

"This made the young men of the village laugh. As they were laughing at Stands Alone, they began to throw stones and sticks at him all the way out of the village where he once called his home.

"Once clear of the village and the young men who were throwing sticks and stones at him, Stands Alone decided that the best place for him to go would be back to his small valley where he had created so many worlds that he could hide in. At least there, he would feel safe and secure once again. At least in this place, he would be wanted because it only existed by his many years of creating it.

"However, when he finally arrived at this place of his, he discovered that it had been completely destroyed. He could imagine who would have done such a thing to him. It had to be those young men of the village that had stoned him out of the village. He made a most sincere promise to himself on that day and on that piece of land. He promised himself that, one day, all of those young men would be made to pay for this pain that they caused him. He knew that in order to do this, he would have to change his ways completely and become a man of power and holdings. To do this, he decided that he would be willing to do anything…at all."

CHAPTER 32

※

Journey to When Spirits Touch

"Stands Alone did not return to his village for many seasons. Season after season, he wandered through other villages that he knew about. Stands Alone was looking for things that would make him a man of power and position so he would be able to return to his own village and show to those young men who had run him out that he was a person that was not to be fooled with.

"In every village that Stands Alone would come to, he would make it his goal to find all of those who had either performed a great quest or had good standing in their village. He would spend much of his youth in serving them. In his mind, this was the way that he would be able to find all of those things in his life path that he felt that he was missing.

"In Stands Alone's mind, he was progressing himself by serving the needs of those others who had a position in their villages. However, in the minds of those he was serving, they made a joke about him and were calling him the servant of others.

"In Stands Alone's mind, he was improving his standing by becoming a serving person to those who had achieved a standing among their own people. At least, he would think this as he would go from one task to the other for them. He was now associating with those who he wanted to be like. It was his way of thinking that if he were to be around them and serve them well, then they would accept him in their own position with their village and he would enjoy these benefits greatly.

"This continued for many seasons. Stands Alone would travel from one village to another. As he was staying in a village that had known him before, he was bringing water to one of the families that he had attached himself to. While he was gathering their water in some pots, he overheard some of the women of the village sharing speaking words about him.

"Since he was kneeling behind a rather large bush, he knew that they would not be able to see him, if he were to remain very quiet. They would not know that he was there and he could hear all of the speaking words that they were sharing about him.

"Stands Alone was expecting to hear them speak of him and all of the tireless efforts that he was making for those of good standing in their village. However, what he was about to hear was not what he had expected.

"'The one who calls himself Stands Alone has returned to our village once again,' said the first woman to the second.

"'Yes, I saw him yesterday. He was gathering wood for two of the families,' said the second woman to the first.

"'I wonder if he knows that even the children have given him a new name?'

"'They have?' replied the second woman, "what are they calling him?'

"'They are calling him The Serving One.'

"'Well, I must admit that this name fits him much better than the one he tells us is his,' came the reply from the second woman.

"'He must have done something very terrible to make him only to seek to serve the needs of others that have been able to accomplish something good in their life path. What do you think?' asked the first woman from the second.

"'I think that he is a very sad man and I take pity on him for the life path he has chosen for himself,' replied the second woman.

"'Why do you take pity on him?' asked the first woman of the second.

"'Because he has no woman and no family. He only wanders from one village to the next and has nothing at all. Sometimes, I will leave a few of our scraps for him in a bowl so that he will at least have something to eat because those who he has given so much service to do not feel as though they have to give anything to him. This makes me very sad for him,' said the second woman to the first.

"'Well, perhaps you are right,' said the first woman. 'I do know that there are no young women of our village that would have anything to do with him. They do not even want to be associated with him and in their gatherings in the evening, they make many laughing songs up about him.'

"'Well, at least he is giving them something to laugh about. So I guess that this life path that he is walking is benefiting a few,' said the second woman.

"'Well,' said the first woman, 'some of those who he has served before say that they consider him to be of less importance than the dogs that we have in our village. They say that he is loyal like a dog but that he requires even less care than a dog because they do not have to feed or care for him.'"

"'So, even the ones who he has been giving his service to do not respect him at all?' asked the second woman.

"'They do not even like him to be around them," replied the first woman. 'They say that the only reason they do not ask him to leave is because they are afraid that they might anger the spirits of the land by being so disrespectful. However, I have heard some of them say that they might be willing to risk this if he comes back into their village again.'

"'This is a very sad man indeed,' replied the second woman, 'I wonder where he will leave his shell when he passes across the great spirit waters?'

"'I can tell you this,' replied the first woman. 'If he leaves it in this village, those who he has served would most likely dump it out on the mesa somewhere and leave it for the crows to eat.'

"Having heard these speaking words from the two women gathered by the water, Stands Alone felt very bad. For all of the things that he thought he was doing to make himself into a more powerful person were only making himself into a person with an even lower standing than he had in his own village when he had left.

"He did not know what to do on this day when he overhead these speaking words. He left the water bowls where they were and decided to leave this village and not ever return. In fact, he decided not to return to any of the villages where he had visited ever again.

"Stands Alone walked away from that village on this day and went out on the mesa to look for a place where he would be able to complete the time that was left to him in the life path that he was walking.

"How wrong he had been in the direction that he had traveled, he was thinking as he walked in his path that led away from the village. How could this have happened to him? How could he have been so wrong?

"As Stands Alone continued walking and asking himself these kinds of questions he finally came upon a friendly looking valley. Here, he thought, was a place where he could live the rest of his time. He saw that there was a small cave on this land and that there was water running over it and there were some small trees and bushes here as well.

"As he surveyed this land he had found, he knew that all of the things that he would need could be provided for him. He walked into this village and began preparing it for himself and his long stay there.

"It was on one of the evenings when Stands Alone was sitting by a fire that he had made for himself when he heard the sounds of approaching footsteps coming in his direction. He picked up one of the long poles that he had designed into a hunting spear and moved himself out of the light so that he might see who or what it was that was approaching his camp."

CHAPTER 33

❀

The Old Man's Speaking Words on the Path to When Spirits Touch

"Out of the darkness, came an old man. Stands Alone could see that this old man could barely walk on his own and he knew that he would not be a threat to him on this night by the fire. As the old man entered into the light so that all of him was very visible, Stands Alone could see that the clothes that he was wearing had about as many seasons on them as did the old man. From what he could see on the old man, he had not eaten much food for at least a season. Feeling a sadness for him, Stands Alone came out of his shadows and into the light of the fire he had built to welcome this old man to his land.

"The old man, seeing Stands Alone come out of the shadows and hearing his greetings, smiled at him and sat himself down by the fire and stared into it silently.

"Stands Alone, not knowing what else to do, sat across from the position where the old man was by his fire and looked into the fire as well."

"'Have you traveled far, old man?' Stands Alone asked.

"'Not nearly as far as you have, young man,' came the reply from the old man. 'And I am sure that for one who has traveled as far as you have that your journey must surely be coming to an end.'

"'I do not travel any longer, old man,' replied Stands Alone. 'This is one thing that I have quit entirely. I only stay in this place where I am appreciated by myself and that is all that I am looking for.'

"'Tell me, how is it that one of so few seasons on their life path with the Earth Mother has become so afraid of others?' the old man asked Stands Alone.

"'What makes you think that I am afraid of others at all, old man?' Stands Alone answered the old man.

"'Why, from just looking at you, I can tell that you have only lived on the outside of yourself. I can tell you that all of those who only have lived on the outside of themselves are always being hurt by others. After many seasons of this, they always become afraid of having anything to do with anyone.'

"Stands Alone looked at the old man. He knew that the old man was correct in his assessment of himself, but he was not aware that it was so obvious that a total stranger could just come and walk into his camp fire and tell him this.

"'It is so obvious to you that you can make this kind of observation about me, old man?'

"'To me, it is very obvious. When you have walked such a long time with the Earth Mother and her children, you cannot help but learn to understand many things that are within her domain,' the old man answered Stands Alone.

"'The old man sat across the fire that was between Stands Alone and him, and stared. 'Would you like to change things, young man?' the old man said, holding both of his hands with their palms up and in front of himself.

"'I have tried to change myself in so many ways, old man. I would be afraid that you would only be wasting your time with one such as me.'

"'If you would like to receive help, young man, you must first be willing to accept it. Do not worry about my time because that is one thing that I have more of than anything else. If you would like to learn how to really change yourself into one who is, then all you have to do is tell me this. If you tell me this, then it will be possible for me to help you. If you do not wish my help, then I am afraid that I must be on my way for there is much work for me to do among the others who also walk a life path such as you do.'

"Stands Alone felt himself being strangely drawn to this old man who had walked into his camp. 'Old man, do I know you from someplace? I have the feeling that I do know you, but I cannot remember from where.'

"The old man looked at Stands Alone and smiled. 'Of course you know me, young man. I have always been here among your people. I have always seen the things that they do. I see all of the things that they will do.'

"'This does not answer your question, Stands Alone. However, you have not used your ears to hear the answer that I have given to you.'

"'Old man, how do you know my name and I do not know yours?' Stands Alone asked, leaning forward towards the fire that was between both of them.

"'You must understand that all things are not as important as others are. This question that you are asking of me is one of those things that are not as important as the one I have asked you,' the old man replied, sitting with his eyes looking deep into the fire now that was before him.

"'I will ask you once again, Stands Alone, do you wish to know the path that will lead you to becoming the person that you wish to be?'

"Stands Alone looked at the old man as he was sitting across the fire from him. He saw that the old man's eyes were fixed on the fire and not on him. This made it very difficult for Stands Alone to feel any meaning that was coming from him. However, since he did not feel anything bad come from him, and he wanted to become the person that he always thought he was, he could only answer yes to the old man.

"'You have made a wise decision, Stands Alone. It is a decision that will benefit you greatly for the rest of the time that is available to you on this life path that you are walking with the Earth Mother.'

"'All I ask of you, in what I am willing to share with you, is that you listen to me very carefully. If there is something that I have shared with you that you do not understand, stop me and I will attempt to explain it better to you. Do you understand this set of instructions that I have given to you?'

"Only shaking his head in an up and down manner, Stands Alone was too shocked by the old man's speaking words to utter any of his own. However, the motion that he was making with his head was enough to let the old man know that he understood what it was that he had asked of him and now he was ready to begin.

"'Very well then, Stands Alone, we shall begin,' the old man said, looking up at the position where Stands Alone was sitting.

"When the old man looked up and Stands Alone saw his eyes, he knew that this was not an ordinary person of the land of the mesa. When he saw the old man's eyes looking at him, they seemed to glow of a clear blue and when he looked into them deeply, he could feel a deep peace come over him.

"'Stands Alone, for all of the life path that you have lived, you have only had one thing in your mind. That was to try to be something that you were not. In the beginning, you believed that you had many people fooled, but they were not fooled by all of your games that you would play with them. In truth, the only person that you were fooling was yourself because many were the times when you actually believed that what you were telling others was truth and this is a very dangerous place for any spirit to be.

"'This not only hurts yourself and the advancement of your spirit, but it will affect all those who are around you. What do you think all of your stories were doing to the ones who thought that they might even be true? Those stories that you were telling of so many great deeds that you were supposed to have done? Do you think that you were giving inspiration to those others who were around you? After all, this is the first reason for our existence. We are supposed to be able to set an example to others by the actions and deeds that we have done...even those who would have eventually become your friend in your village. When you were telling them of all the great things that you were doing, what do you think that this was doing to them?

"'I will tell you that all of the stories you had told them were actually stopping them from attempting to do those things for themselves. Your stories were stopping them from trying, because they felt that they would not ever be able to perform those things that you said you had done. When they would compare their deeds to the ones that you told them that you had done, theirs seemed to be so small that they decided that it was not worth it to even try.

"'What you were doing by telling these stories to the others of your village was not at all what you had intended to do, Stands Alone. Instead of making a place for yourself in your village, you had stopped the advancement and growth of not only your own spirit, but also of those spirits who were listening to you.

"'When those others saw that there was no spiritual advancement in you, they knew that something had to be wrong with what you were telling them. You see, when a spirit who is walking a life path with the Earth Mother is successful in accomplishing such tasks or quests, then they are blessed not only by the Earth Mother but also by the spirits of the land. These blessings become obvious to all that will ever cast their eyes on them.

"'In your case, as you continued to tell your stories to those of the village, and they saw that there was no advancement in your spirit, they knew that something was wrong. Do not blame those young men of the village for doing what they had done to you. Had they not heard such words from you, they would not have ever done such a thing. However, since the wise ones of your village saw the harm that you were doing by telling your stories to those others who would listen to you, they had decided that the best thing for the entire village would be to ask you to leave and not come back until you had more spirit within you.

"'If you have anyone to put blame on, Stands Alone, it is only yourself. All this happened to you because you were trying to be someone who you were not. You were not willing to put forth the effort that was needed to be who you said you were. Even though all of the village had turned against you, you had, and still have, one true friend who is still there. That one is Wind Song. She was the only one who held you in a place of the heart and spoke to you as she did. Had you listened to her on that day she followed you out of the village and onto the mesa, you would not be so lonely now. At least you would have her to stand beside you in your times of need.

"'However, instead of listening to this one friend that you have made, you decided to leave everything behind and let vengeance take you for its ride. Let me tell you, Stands Alone, there is only one spirit that rules this vengeance. The name of this spirit is One Who feels Pity For Themselves. This spirit took you the way that it is very familiar with and led you from one village to another. Some of the villages you have travel through are not even known to the members of your village. However, instead of listening to the wise words of your friend, Wind Song, you listened to this spirit of vengeance and were hoping to find an easy way to get back at all of those young men of your village.

"'It is unfortunate that you have taken this path. This spirit of vengeance has robbed you of many seasons of your growing time. This spirit has closed you off to all things that were inside of you and has stopped you from learning anything from any of the places and things you have done. If you had continued on this path, you would have ended up as a very angry spirit. When you would eventually arrive at the waiting place across the great spirit waters, and found out that you had accomplished nothing at all during this life path that you had been offered, you would have known the term sadness.

"'Think about those things that you did next in all of those villages that you had gone into. You went into these places picking out those others who had accomplished great things and held a good place in the village where they were living. You thought that by doing many things for them that you would find favor from them. However, this is not how such a thing works. If one, who has been able to accomplish quests successfully for the Earth Mother and her children, is close to you, then rest assured that they will have all been blessed with the eyes of the spirit to see. They saw you for what you were trying to do with them. The you that they saw was the worst kind of thief that there could be. This kind of thief tries to steal from the spirit who is traveling forward. This thief will do all that it can do to stop their advancement by placing many obstacles in their way. This is what you were doing in those far off places that you had traveled to, Stands Alone. You were not being accepted by any of these others. In fact, had you not left these villages when you did, you would have found that they, too, would have asked you to leave them and not to ever come back.

"'So, Stands Alone, the path that you were traveling would have brought you to this place where you are at now whether you would have chosen to do so or not. In time, you would have had no other place left for you to go and even your one friend would have forgotten you. What you have succeeded in doing is to put a great shell around you. This shell closed off all who would come to you and had even closed off your own spirit from reaching you. This shell has left you completely empty of all things of value. It was not possible for you to know that such things even existed.'

"The old man looked into the face of Stands Alone and what he saw brought him to a sad heart. There, sitting silently in front of the small fire that he had built for this night was Stands Alone spilling much water from both of his eyes. The old man knew that he had reached the spirit of Stands Alone and then offered him some speaking words that would bring him some comfort for this night that they were sharing together.

"'All is not lost, Stands Alone. There is still time for you in this life path that you are walking with the Earth Mother and her children. There is still time for you to reclaim this one true friend of yours if you would but follow my advice in what I will tell you,' the old man continued.

"'Will you be willing to do this for yourself, Stands Alone?' the old man asked.

"'Yes,' came the trembling voice of Stands Alone, across the small fire that he had built for this night.

"'Then listen to me very well, Stands Alone. For these things that I am willing to share with you have not been given to many who are walking a life path with the Earth Mother and for this, you should feel very proud.

"'You must remember that there will not ever be anything that you will be able to claim as your own in this life path without working for it. The kind of work that you will be required to do will be to go into the silence with me. You must learn this spirit very well. By doing this, you will find those things that you are looking for. In this place will be all of the things of the spirit that will assist you to learn. They will help you in gaining the understanding that will assist you in getting back onto the correct path. The path that you should have been on many seasons ago.'

"The old man got up from his seated position and walked over to sit next to where Stands Alone was sitting. He spoke to him of the way that their traveling would take place. He began singing a spirit song for him to follow as he began his traveling within himself.

"The old man stayed with Stands Alone for many days and nights. Each day and each night, the old man would take Stands Alone into the silence where he would learn many things…things which helped him to understand why he had walked a path as he had done. He taught him to accept himself for who he was and to understand those things that were himself.

"With the passing of one complete season, Stands Alone was no longer the one he had been before. He was now a new person and one who knew himself. He understood that all things that would be accomplished in this life path of his would have to be done by him…that it would be he who would be completely responsible for all of the things that he was to do.

"He learned many things in this one season that he had spent with the old man. One of the things that he came to understand was that it would be necessary for him to go back to all of the places where he had once visited and explain to all of those others who he had tried to rob what he had done and ask for their forgiveness, or at least their understanding.

"The old man smiled at Stands Alone when he told him this. The old man told him that he was ready to continue with his life path on his own. He told Stands Alone that he was very proud of him for being able to reach the correct path once again and that he was sure that instead of bringing much hurt to other spirits, that he would bring them great joy and help.

"'My time here with you is over now. I am called to other places to offer my assistance to those who have found the same kind of path that you were on,' the old man said, as he rose from his position that he was in.

"As he was walking out of the small camp, Stands Alone suddenly jumped up and said, 'Old man, for this season that we have spent together, I have not come to learn what your name is so that I may include you in my prayers of thanks to the Earth Mother and the Great Spirit.'

"'I am called Tree,' came the words from the old man, as he turned around to have one last look on the face of Stands Alone. 'I will not ever be far away from you in the life path that you walk. Stay on the correct path now that you have found it. When you see another who has gotten lost like you have, take the time to let them know the correct path by your deeds, and not by your words alone.'

"When Tree had finished his speaking words to Stands Alone, he turned and walked off into the hills that were around them. Stands Alone did not ever see Tree again but he included him in all of his prayers and held him close in all of his thoughts for the rest of the time that was his to share with the Earth Mother and her children."

CHAPTER 34

❀

The Journey Back to When Spirits Touch

"For the next seven seasons, Stands Alone went to village after village that he had been to before. In each of the villages, he would speak to each person who he had affected by his actions and had asked for their forgiveness and understanding. In those villages, he also assisted many of the others who were living there in understanding the way to the correct path. His teachings went far and wide among all of the people he would visit.

"Finally, Stands Alone had been to all of the villages he had visited before. When he was done with the last of them, the speaking words of Tree came back to him. He remembered how Tree would always tell him how much better he would feel in his body and in his spirit when he had completed this quest of his. Now, Stands Alone was ready to travel to his own village. Here, he would also speak to all those others who had been affected by his stories and ask for their forgiveness and understanding.

"It took Stands Alone almost one complete season to reach the village where he had begun his life path with. It took him such a long time because everywhere he would go, there would be others who would seek him out for the wisdom of his teachings and he would not ever turn away another who was in need.

"As he continued with his traveling, he found that there were many who had taken up their path with his and would walk with him so that they would always know where he would be. When he finally reached his village, he had many dozens of others who were following him because they were still in a stage of learning about the silence and what the correct path was from him.

"He had paused on the outside of his own village and there, standing before him, was his one true friend. It was Wind Song. Seeing Stands Alone, she came running across the land to greet him.

"'I am filled with a great joy in seeing you on our lands once again, Stands Alone,' Wind Song said, as she pulled herself up very close to him.

"'I am filled with as much joy in seeing that you are still here in the village and that you remember me, Wind Song,' Stands Alone said.

"'I am here to explain to all those of our village what bad things that I had done to them and to ask for their forgiveness and understanding,' Stands Alone continued with the speaking words that he was sharing.

"'That will not be necessary now,' Wind Song said, as she was busy looking into the eyes of Stands Alone. 'Our people have heard of the great works that you have been sharing with other villages and we are all very proud of you. By your actions, the forgiveness and understanding that you are seeking has been given to you long ago. Now all of our people are ready to welcome you back into this village and give to you a place of great honor where you may sit.'

"'Come with me,' Wind Song said aloud to Stands Alone, and all those who were with him. 'Come with me, all of you, and let our village do you great honor,' Wind Song said, with a great smile crossing over her face and walking as if she were on a cloud into the direction of their village.

"When they arrived at the village, all of the members came forward and greeted Stands Alone and welcomed him and those others who had come with him. They had all shared a great feast and the elder of the village rose and showed Stands Alone a new place that had been built for them all to live.

"'When one who is so greatly respected among so many comes to live in our village, then it is expected that there will always be many who will seek him out to gain their insight from his words of wisdom. Look to where I am pointing and you will see that there have been a great number of new lodgings for all of you. These places will be for you and those who will come among us seeking your words of wisdom in the teachings that you will give to them.

"'We are honored to welcome you and all who will come to you in this our gift to the things that you will teach to our people and our people's people.'

"Having finished the great feast and finding that he and his following would be welcomed in his own village. Stands Alone walked out to the land of the mesa once again to be alone. He knew that he had come such a long way with his spirit. It made him feel very good. When he got to the same place where his one friend, Wind Song, had met him before, he found that she was there once again and was looking at him with a large and tender smile that was covering her face.

"'I knew that you would come back to us one day, Stands Alone,' she said, as she continued to look into his eyes. 'Now though, there is something different that lives within you that I did not ever see before. It is something that draws me to you much like the fire draws the small things of the night to it.'

"'Yes,' came the words from Stands Alone. 'I, too, see this new thing that lives within you as well, and I, too, am drawn into it.'

"'What can this thing be, Stands Alone?' Wind Song asked, with her eyes still fixed on his.'

"'I can only say this, Wind Song. I believe that what we see in the other one was always there from the very beginning. However, since I was not ready to see it, then it was passing me by. Now that it has shown itself to me, I know that it is something that I will look for with great joy if I am allowed to be with you each day for the rest of the life path that I am walking with the Earth Mother.'

"'I also feel this way, Stands Alone. It is like we have always known each other for longer than we have been with the Earth Mother. I feel such a warm and knowing feeling from you now but it was not there before for me either. However, it is here now, and I too would consider it to be a great blessing from the Earth Mother if I were to be allowed to share this with you for each day that is left to the life path that I am walking.'

"In each life path, there is always one who will make a difference in arriving at the path we are seeking. For me, it was Tree and I will tell you more about him as time passes for both of us. Tell me, Wind Song, who has it been for you?' Stands Alone asked, as he continued looking deep into her eyes.

"Only one word came forth from her lips to Stands Alone at that time and on that place: 'You.'

"From that day on, both of them shared the remainder of the life path together. All, who would come close to them, as they continued to share the wisdom of their teachings, would feel the greatness of the love that lived between them. And feeling this love, they too were blessed because they could not only learn from the speaking words that Stands Alone would share with them, but they would be able to feel what this love shared between two spirits felt like.

"Their entire village prospered for the time that was left to Stands Alone and Wind Song. All things that they would endeavor to do would be done very well. All of the animals and plants that were close to their village would prosper. When others would come seeking the wisdom of Stands Alone, they only had to look for the place within the domain of the Earth Mother's where life was always growing and giving all who would cross over it its peace and love of balance.

"Before Stands Alone and Wind Song left the domain of the Earth Mother and crossed over the great spirit waters to the waiting place, they left a spirit painting for all who would be willing to see to learn from. This is what I have brought the both of you here to see. The one who I have left the loaf of bread stuffed into this small hole in the rock is Tree. He will be able to see that we not only remember his beginning teachings that Stands Alone left to us, but that we also remember that when we leave something for the children of the Earth Mother to eat, then she too will be happy. This will help in attaining the balance that Tree had taught to Stands Alone those many generations ago."

CHAPTER 35

❀

The Shell That Holds

Grandfather got up from the position where he had been seated and told us to follow him into the cave so that we would be able to share this thing of beauty that Stands Alone and Wind Song left for us.

We got up from the positions that we had been seated in and followed Grandfather into the cave. As we began our walk through the cave, he handed each of us a torch that he lit for us.

"These torches will not make any smoke but they will go out easily. Make sure that if yours begin to go out, let me know and I will arrange the sticks so that they will be able to lit once again."

Finishing his speaking words to us, he made a motion that we should stay where we were until our eyes could adjust to this new source of light. Grandfather told us that there would be places in this cave that would cause us to fall if we could not see where it was that we were walking.

It was only a matter of minutes before our eyes adjusted to this light. Now, we were ready to continue with our direction into the cave.

As we went into this cave, we could tell that there had been many others who had traveled this way. Some of the places where we would walk were only a stone bottom and there had been, from many seasons of others passing this way, grooves that were cut into the stone pathway.

On the way to the back of this cave, we passed many places where we could have fallen. In the path that we were walking, there had been places that appeared to be large holes in the floor. We could tell that at one time, there had been great stones there, but for whatever reason that there was, they had been taken out and nothing was put into the places where they had once been.

Grandfather was turning around to see if we were still following him as he continued through the cave. "Be careful not to lose my light," came his speaking words to us. "There are many other passages that have been built into this great stone that we are in."

Just as he said this, Cheeway and I heard the sound of water running. When we turned our lights to it, we saw that there was another passage that led off in another direction. Not wanting to stay in our positions any longer, we continued to follow Grandfather's light. It was now very far ahead of us.

Very soon, we saw that he had stopped and had turned around to look in the direction that we were coming from. We could see that he was in a room of some kind because there did not seem to be a top or side visible to us as we continued to walk toward him.

Reaching the room, he held out his left hand and pointed to a place on one of the walls where he wanted us to look. When we turned our heads in the direction, we saw that there was a very large spirit painting on the face of the stone in this room that we were in.

Pointing at a place on the spirit painting where one old man was standing, Grandfather said, "Here is Tree."

Grandfather then took our torches from our hands and placed them in positions near the spirit painting so that the light could light it up almost as bright as the sun would have done if this place had been on the outside of the cave.

Once he had placed the torches in their places, he motioned to both of us to have a seat just behind the torches.

"The old man that you see in this spirit painting is Tree. He is the one I told you both about. He was the one who began many of the teachings that we live with even in this generation that we are in."

Cheeway and I looked at the spirit painting and could see that there were other people in it as well. We saw that there was a man standing and a woman sitting. Around the man was some kind of a bubble that was cracked open and he had walked through it. Behind him were many people and some of them were standing while others of them were sitting. All of them had the same kind of a bubble around them, and for the most part, they were cracked open with them walking out of it.

CHAPTER 36

❀

When the Spirit Gains Freedom to See

We could see that those who had walked out of the bubble thing that was around them were smiling, while those who seemed to still be in theirs were holding a face that did not look good at all. We did not understand these things that were on the spirit painting and asked Grandfather to explain them in more detail to the both of us.

"You both remember how I told you that Stands Alone had tired to discover the secret of himself through the actions of others?"

"Yes, Grandfather," we both said, sitting in the front of the spirit painting. "We remember how you told us that all that Stands Alone was doing was to go to the outside of himself to look and this was why he was so unsuccessful in discovering who he really was."

"This spirit painting that you are both looking at was done by Stands Alone and Wind Song spirit helpers. It was while they were lying in their death robes that they instructed one of the villagers that when they had finally crossed over the great spirit waters and had gone to the waiting place, that they should go into the cave that we are in and look on the wall of the far room.

"Once they had left our lands of the mesa and the domain of the Earth Mother, two of the villagers had come into the cave where we are and had seen this spirit painting. They informed the others of the village that the spirit helpers of Stands Alone and Wind Song had performed this great thing.

"One by one, all those who were in the village on that day came by this spirit painting and looked deeply at it so that they could understand more of the depth of its meaning to them. All of the people who you see behind the standing man, who is Stands Alone, and the sitting woman, who is Wind Song, have been added to by those same spirits.

"When this spirit painting was first completed, there were only three others who were standing behind them. Now, as you can see, there are many others who are standing behind them."

"Did those of the village come and paint over this spirit painting, Grandfather?" Cheeway asked, as he was sitting next to me.

"No one in their correct spirit would ever do such a thing, Cheeway. This would be considered one of the greatest insults not only to the Earth Mother and the spirits of the land, but to the Great Spirit as well. However, in the beginning, and while the village of ruins was still standing, there were those who thought that this was the case, and that someone who was not of good spirit was doing this.

"Each night, there were two people placed to guard against any kind of actions like this happening. But with the passing of a few seasons, and without any further clues as to who was doing this, there appeared more and more pictures of others who were standing behind Stands Alone and Wind Song.

"Over the passing of these seasons, the ones who had been there to watch for such things had nothing to tell about. To each of them, there were no others in the caves when these new people appeared on the spirit painting. It was then that they knew that the addition of others who were being included in this spirit painting were done by the spirit helpers of Tree, Stands Alone, and Wind Song."

"Grandfather,' I asked, still sitting in the same position that I had been in. "With such a great spirit painting such as this, why did the village move away?"

"It has always been the way of our people to allow the spirits of the land enough freedom to do what it is that they must do. Our people knew that if they were to stay in this village and in such close place to a living spirit painting, the temptation to have others come to it and ruin it would be great. The entire village decided that for them to leave this land and allow the memory of the location of this spirit painting for only the wise ones to remember would be the best thing for all of them to do. Also, it would give the spirits, who were continuing to add to this spirit painting, the freedom to accomplish that which they had been guided to do.

"This is why this once great village where Stands Alone and Wind Song once lived was allowed to be returned to the Earth Mother. What you have walked through was, at one time in the history of our people, one of the greatest villages that had ever been seen on the land of the mesa. However, because of the great sacrifice that was made by those who lived in this village, the Earth Mother blessed them greatly and gave them land where the life that they needed was abundant."

"But, Grandfather," I asked. "How did they ever get all of the people of the village to move at one time and agree not to return to this place where their families were born?"

"You must remember, little one, that there is one thing that is stronger than anything you will ever encounter in this life path you are walking with the Earth Mother. That thing is when it is time for something to occur, then nothing will ever stand in its way. It was time for this to happen and all of the people of the village knew it. For them, it was not a difficult task. For them, it was simply a task that had to be done because it was time."

"Grandfather," Cheeway asked.

"Yes, Cheeway, what is it?" Grandfather returned.

"What about those bubbles that are drawn around many of those who are in the spirit painting? Will you also tell us of them?"

"These bubbles that you refer to are the picture symbol of the shell that we all can have around us. This shell is developed when we are not sure of ourselves and we put this all around ourselves so that no hurt may pass through it.

"However, what we do not see is that while no hurt may pass through this shell that we have created, it will not allow anything else to pass through it either. This includes anything passing out of it so that it may be shared with others."

"But, Grandfather," I said, "if this shell is so bad on the advancement of understanding of the life path we are walking, then why do so many others keep it with them?"

"First, you must understand that there are always two ways of looking at all things that come to you. There is the way of looking at yourself from a position that another may see you. This way is usually the most beneficial in making the determination of what things that you have are good and which things that you have are not so good.

"The second way of looking at ourselves is the most common of ways. That is to see ourselves with only our own eyes. These eyes can fool us from time to time if we are not aware of what things to look for.

"The greatest reason that so many others keep this shell around them is that they are fooled by those eyes of themselves. What they see when they look upon this shell that they have put around themselves is something that makes them invulnerable enough that they seem very tough in the face of all things that may come to them in their life path.

"Since they see this shell only with their own eyes, they only see that since they cannot be hurt, then they must be able to pass through anything that may confront them. And since they feel that they cannot be hurt by these things, then they believe that this shell is a good thing. Instead of getting rid of it and exposing themselves to all of the pain and hurt that may come their way, they decide to strengthen it even more. They believe that this is what makes them appear strong to all others with whom they come into contact with.

"When others will see them, they will not perceive them as strong at all. They will see through this shell of theirs, if they have the inner eyes that the spirit brings to us, and they will see a very frightened person who only makes bad decisions about all things that may come their way.

"So you see, these people who have this shell around them, cannot see through it as they continue to grow it stronger and stronger around them. They cannot see the truth in the way that they are walking their life path. They only see themselves as one who cannot be hurt or affected by anything that comes their way. Because of this, all of the decisions that they make are actually very bad and wrong ones. They cannot see themselves in the light of the spirit of truth; they only see themselves as being the best one to make any decisions there are to be made. They perceive themselves to be above any emotion that may cloud their decision making.

"In truth, what others see in those who have embraced this shell of theirs, is a person who is so far away from the truth of anything that no matter what it is that they will do, say, or decide, it will always be wrong. They do not possess the understanding that is needed in order to make a good decision. These wise ones who have the eyes of the spirit will stay away from those with the shells around them. The ones with the shells around them will stay away from the wise ones because they believe themselves as too good to associate with them.

"So, you see, this truth that is embraced within this spirit painting shows many others breaking away from their shells and walking through them. And as they are walking through them, they are wearing a very happy face and with a smile. They know that what they have done is good and while they may be exposed to the pain and hurt that is all around each of us, they will also see the goodness and the joy that is next to them as well.

"It is very unfortunate that those who are living their life path within these shells cannot see this. Because when they have stopped the hurt and pain from coming in, they have also blocked out all of the goodness and learning that will lead them to the path of understanding. You see, no spirit may succeed with the life path that they are walking with the Earth Mother without encountering all of these feelings. It is by learning to work through them that we are able to learn. This is the only way that we will advance our spirits. This is the only reason that we have come to the Earth Mother to walk a life path. This is what we must learn to work through."

"Grandfather," Cheeway said, "then why are there those others who are shown in the spirit painting who still have their shell around them?"

"Cheeway, just look at the faces that they have on them. Can you see how sad they look especially when you compare them to those who have broken out of their shells?"

"Yes, I can see this," Cheeway responded.

"This is why they have been included in this spirit painting. They are there to remind you of the difference in the way we would be with and without the shell that goes around the body that our spirit travels in.

"Now let us spend the rest of the time that we have in this place in opening our minds and our spirits to all those things that are within this spirit painting of our people. Take the time to travel with the spirit of silence as you do this and you will find that there will be many more truths that will come to you from this spirit painting."

For the rest of the time that we shared in this cave with the spirit painting, we all three sat in silence and looked for other hidden truths. Grandfather had shared much with us on this day and both Cheeway and I were sure that it would take us much time to sort through all of what had been shared with us. For all that we had shared on this day, both Cheeway and I were feeling very good. We knew that Grandfather had spent much time with us in sharing his speaking words.

Some of the speaking words that were coming to me as I went into the spirit of silence were: "Whenever a spirit, who is attempting to learn, encounters others who are also attempting to learn, then there is a great freedom to grow. Here in this place, where they will gather, shall there be great advancements in their spirits. It is this freedom of truth and acceptance that will allow this growth and advancement to come forth. All who will accept it will know truth. These will be the things you will take with you when it comes time for you to cross over the great spirit waters to the waiting place.

"Once there, all of those times that you have shared with other spirits who were attempting to advance themselves will be shared and known by all who are among your spirit family. They will be glad that this has happened. Appreciate these times when they come to you. If you do this, then you will not miss them when they are gone. You will continue to grow because they have become a part of you."

PART XI

❀

A GATHERING OF VISIONS

CHAPTER 37

❀

Journey to the Jemez Mountains

Grandfather had taken Cheeway and I to one of our villages in the Jemez Mountains. These mountains are in the northern part of the State of New Mexico. We would always look forward to traveling with him to these places. Each time that we would travel with him to one of these villages, we would find that there was always many kinds of games and other kids our own age that we could play with.

We had left very early in the morning and, as was usual for both Cheeway and myself, we would sleep for the majority of the ride. I would remember Grandfather always telling us both, that if we would be allowed to, that we could sleep away at least half of our life path that we were walking.

This day in the front of Grandfather's truck was no different for both of us and as the sun slowly crossed over the thin line of darkness that covered our lands, it found us both asleep.

Grandfather was taking us to one of the smaller villages in the Jemez where he was going to meet Two Bears and one other of his long time friends. From that village, we would travel into the mountains where there was going to be a great ceremony in which we would give our thanks to the Earth Mother for all that she had done for us this season.

Cheeway and I were looking forward to this part of the trip because it meant that we would both be able to ride in the back part of Grandfather's truck where we could feel the wind rush across us. In times such as these, we would often pretend that we were small eagles flying across our lands and this gave us a good feeling.

Grandfather did not mind us doing this kind of playing as long as we stayed seated in the back of the truck. However we, as did many of the other children who would ride in the back of trucks, had to learn the hard way that what he had told us was for our own good. We had almost fallen out of the truck when we were playing this game. Fortunately for both of us, he was not going very fast. This was enough of a scare for both Cheeway and I to remember that we must stay seated all of the time that we were in the back of the truck.

Thinking back on the time when we almost fell out of the truck though, I am not so sure that he did not plan to scare us that day. However, for whatever reason there was, it had been sufficient for us to know that to maintain a position that was not a seated one was very dangerous and we did not ever try that again.

We had asked Grandfather about the identity of this other person that we were going to pick up along with Two Bears in the small village in the Jemez. He just looked at us and smiled as he told us that this was another person that he had grown up with but had not seen for many years. Since he was not willing to share any more information with us at this time, we knew better than to ask him more and decided to drop the subject entirely.

I was suddenly awakened from my sleep in the front of the truck by the sounds of others sharing speaking words and laughter. As I opened my eyes, I saw that we were already in the small mountain village and he and two others were standing on the outside of the truck sharing things that brought them great joy.

One of the men I recognized as Two Bears and it made my heart feel very good to see him once again. However, the other man I did not know. He looked friendly enough, but I knew that I had not seen him before. However, I did have the feeling within me that I should know him.

I shook Cheeway who was laying across the seat. As usual, Cheeway could only look at me after coming out of the world with the dream spirit. I knew better than to ask him to speak for at least twenty minutes after he would wake up. It was not that he did not want to share speaking words with anyone, it was simply that he could not. He had always been like this and I knew what to expect. Grandfather had always told us both that in order for a good friendship to grow among any two people, then there must be the certainty that the other's ways are known so they are not offensive to you. In this way, Cheeway and I had always known of many things about each other, and it was because of this that we had been so successful in growing our friendship.

"Get up, Cheeway," I said to him, as I continued to shake one of his legs that was close to me. "We are here and Grandfather is already outside of the truck sharing speaking words with the two that will be coming with us."

Cheeway could only look at me with his one open eye. He lifted his head and saw that what I had told him to be true. Suddenly, and for him it was sudden, he began to move from where he was. However, his body did not know where or what he wanted to do and it was going off in many directions at the same time.

I knew that I would have to do something before I would end up with one of his feet in my face.

"Cheeway!" I said, holding onto his leg that was the closest to me. "Tell me what direction you are wanting to go in and perhaps I will be able to help you."

With both of his eyes half open, Cheeway could only point to the back of the truck. I knew that this was where he was trying to go, but his body seemed to wake up just about as badly as he did. Because of this, Cheeway was almost dysfunctional after coming back from the dream spirits.

I helped him up and out of the cab of the truck. When Grandfather, Two Bears, and the man saw us coming out, they all three gave us their morning greetings. We managed to return them and quickly got into the back of the truck where there were blankets for us to cover up in and continue our visit with the dream spirits.

It was not until we had traveled many miles that we both woke up. When we looked out of the back of the truck, and from under the blankets that were over us, we could see that we were in a high place in the mountains already. We knew that we had missed much of the scenery that we had wanted to see. In order to make up for this, we began playing our games that would take place within our minds.

Grandfather had always taught us that the best way to entertain oneself is to find games to play that would go along with the setting that we were in. In this case, we had decided to set our games in observing those things of the Earth Mother that were taking place around us.

When I looked over at the place where Cheeway was, I could see that he had already begun his game. By the look that was on his face, he was far away from this place where his body was resting. Seeing this, I laid back on the floor of the truck bed and looked up at the gathering of clouds that were coming across these lands of ours.

As I laid back on the bed of the truck, I allowed my mind to wander with the wind spirit as he was moving the clouds across that deep blue sky that was always over our lands. I found myself drifting with the movements of the truck that was beneath me and the clouds that were over me.

Each time Grandfather would make another turn with the truck, I could feel myself becoming lighter and lighter, as I would follow the path of the clouds that were over me. As this process continued, I found that I was listening to many voices chanting. At first, I did not know where they were coming from, but as time passed, I could tell that they were coming from the clouds that were above me. Or at least they were coming from that general direction.

I allowed myself to drift into this world that was being shown to me. I could tell that this was one of the edges of one of many spirit worlds that were available to us when we would reach a certain point of spiritual development and I wanted to see what it would show to me.

Laying back in the truck, I could let myself go into the sounds that were coming to me more and more. Grandfather's turning of the truck would help me to attain a position that went even closer to this spirit world edge than I had been able to ever get before. As I allowed my spirit to continually rise to this place where I could hear the chanting coming from, I could make out that there were what appeared to be many spirits walking through the clouds that were above our lands.

They seemed to be walking in unison to the chanting that was being delivered to me on the back of the wind spirit. As I continued to look at the clouds, they were taking on the form of many who had once walked a life path with the Earth Mother.

Continuing to observe this event, I could hear that the chanting was becoming louder now and was echoing off of the walls of the mountains that were surrounding us. As Grandfather continued to drive his truck into the direction of the place where the great ceremony was going to be held, I looked up at the clouds that were spread over us and I could see what appeared to be many spirits walking in the shadow of the shells that they once had while walking a life path with the Earth Mother.

Watching them, I could see that they were all heading in the same direction as we were. They appeared to be going to the place where the great ceremony was being held.

As they continued to walk their path across the skies that were over our lands, I could hear the sounds of chanting getting louder. Also, within the sounds of chants, I could hear the sounds of drums being played and the spirit caller's bells being rung. It was then that I realized that all of these sounds that were making me relax so much were coming from the place where we were going. However, as I continued to recognize these sounds as being from our people in the ceremonial place, the spirits' forms in the clouds that were above me did not go away. They continued to walk into the same direction. When Grandfather had stopped his truck and told us that we were here, I could see that all of the spirits in the clouds above us were beginning to gather and were staying in the skies that were above this place.

How wonderful, I thought to myself, that so many spirits would come to visit us on our lands and on this special occasion. Giving them a last glance before getting out of the back of the truck, I could tell that many of them seemed to be laying on their stomachs and were looking down on all of the thankful things that were being said and done by our people on these lands. I received the feeling that all of our efforts were pleasing to them on this day.

When Cheeway and I got out of the back of the truck, we saw that we were the youngest ones here. All of those who were giving thanks to the Earth Mother on this day were much older than we were. Most of them seemed to have the same number of seasons on them as Grandfather and Two Bears did.

However, this did not bother either of us all that much. We were used to being around many others who were not of our age. Grandfather would always tell us that it was better to be able to learn how to enjoy the times that you have, rather than feel bad about those times that were not with you. This would give each of us an advantage in the life path that we were walking. It would teach us to look for those things that were presented to us, no matter what they were, so that we could learn from them.

Grandfather had always told us that there would not ever be anything that would be presented to either of us that would not have a specifically designed reason for it. If we would learn to look for the things that were presented, we could learn to understand the reason that they were near us. Then, as we would gather more seasons in our life path, we would understand more of what would come to us.

Looking to see what had happened to Grandfather, Two Bears, and their friend, we saw that they had taken up a position in the inner circle of the ceremonial place where they were sharing speaking words with others who they knew.

Cheeway and I took up a place on one of the tall rocks that was in this land where we could sit above all of the larger heads that were around us and still be able to see and hear what was being done in the middle of the ceremonial circle.

CHAPTER 38

Song of the Spirit Caller

On this day, there was one who was a spirit caller from one of the mountain villages in the Jemez Mountains. He was singing a spirit chant that would be close to a lullaby to wake up with. These singing words that he was sharing with the council members, the Earth Mother, the spirits of the land, and the children of the Earth Mother were ones that were telling all of them that the time for the sleeping season was almost over now and it was time for them to come back to these lands.

His singing words were such that it would even make a child smile as they were waking up from their nightly visit with the dream spirits. Hearing his singing words, both Cheeway and I were feeling the life fill both of us up so much that we felt like jumping up and down with the joy of being alive.

We knew that those others who were also in attendance at this ceremony were feeling the same way. When he had finished his singing words, there was a brief silence. Then there was a loud cry of "Wahoop!", which was the sound of combining the small child within us and the adult that we all hope to be. By this signal, all who would hear it would know that it was time to let all of the emotions and feelings out as they would dance to the sounds of the singers and drum players.

It was by this kind of release that all who were present would cleanse themselves of the feelings that had come alive within them by the spirit caller's song.

When the cleansing was completed, all became seated once again and prepared themselves to listen to the next one who would come before them with another message or blessing that had been given to them to share.

Since it was a part of our peoples' custom not to take more time than was necessary to convey their message, the spirit caller sat down in the place that had been marked for him within the circle. All of our people hold the value of being one's self in a very high esteem so it was only natural for him to be seated because he did not know who else had been given a message to deliver.

As Cheeway and I continued to observe all that was taking place within this ceremonial circle, we were very surprised to see that the next one of our people who was getting up to address this ceremonial group was Grandfather.

CHAPTER 39

❀

Grandfather's Message

When Grandfather got up from his sitting position and entered the center of the inner circle, all that were in attendance at this ceremony became very quiet. It was as though they knew what he was going to share with them held great weight.

As we saw Grandfather commanding such great respect among those others at this ceremony, we were very proud of him and sat in our positions of the large rock with both of our chests pushed out. Looking in the direction where Two Bears and their friend were sitting, we could see that they were looking at the both of us and were wearing a large smile over their faces. We knew that they too were very proud for what Grandfather was going to share with this ceremonial council.

As we saw Grandfather enter into the center of the circle, he made a motion with his right hand. This motion was held in an outward position and had his palm at first face up then turned faced sideways. All who would see this motion would know that this meant that these speaking words that he was about to share with them were from the Earth Mother. Those who would hear them would be responsible for sharing them with others of their own villages.

The silence was broken after Grandfather had made a complete circle so that he would be able to see that all that were present in this place had seen him. This was important when one had a message that was to be shared with so many in attendance.

"Listen to these messages that I have for all who are here with me. These messages come to me from the Earth Mother and the spirits of the land as well as from our ancestors who are with us all in this ceremonial place.

"Those who have come here on this day have come to do the Earth Mother a great honor by showing her gratitude for all of the blessings that she has bestowed on us. Those who have come among us know that the messages we bring here are not from ourselves, but they are from those who have gone before us and are here to help us in the greatest quest of all…to advance our spirits to a place where we can once again become one with the Great Spirit.

"The life paths that we are all walking among the children of the Earth Mother are not new to many of us. Most of us have been through this path of hers before and most of us will be back once again. However, what I have come here to announce is that all of the times that we and many of our generations that have come before us have known…will not return for many seasons."

Grandfather paused for a brief moment to allow his speaking words to sink into the ones who were present to hear them. We could hear many voices sharing their surprise at what they had heard as Grandfather's message opened. All who knew him, we could see by the looks that they had placed over their faces, knew that speaking words that he shared with them were not ever given lightly, nor were they ever said without a sureness to understand them first before he would share them with any of our people.

Because of this, all those who were in attendance at this council were shocked. When their low speaking voices were cleared, he continued.

"I am not speaking of the time when those who were not of our people fenced us into lands and stopped our freedom among the Earth Mother and her children. I am not here to tell you of a kind of fence like that. This fence has only kept those who built it out. It did not serve any purpose at keeping us in.

"We who have attained the levels of understanding that comes from remembering the wisdom of our peoples' past realize that we were the ones who could go in and out from this fenced area of ours. Those who had built these fences could do neither one. It was we who were able to live on both sides of the fence when it suited our needs; those who built it could only stay on the outside of it.

"For those generations that have passed our people, we have seen that our ways have been protected. We have seen to it that our people would learn the ways of the old while putting up with the ways of the new. We knew that we had to give and take from the times that were upon us.

"However, there is a new fence that is required to be built now. It will be our own people who will build this fence. It will be our own people who will make sure that it is kept up and only a few who will be able to cross it…ever."

Now, as Cheeway and I looked over the group of our people who had gathered in this ceremonial circle, we could see that the looks of shock that was on their faces had turned into ones of fear. All who were present knew what the reference to the fence was. All present knew that the times that are referred to as the time of the fence meant that a completely new way of managing our life paths had come to us. Grandfather was telling them that there was a need for a new fence to be built and by our own people.

We could see that these looks of fear that were on our people's faces were also being shared by Two Bears and their friend. We could also feel that this look was on our faces as well. There was not one other person in this whole gathering that did not have their attention focused on the speaking words that Grandfather was about to share with all of them.

"The past several seasons of this life path that I have been walking have been spent in great study. I have devoted much of my time, since my other half has crossed the great spirit waters to the waiting place, in listening and increasing my understanding of all the messages that have been given to me.

"I have been charged by Two Elks and Morning Wind to undertake this quest. Now, the time is right to share some of these things with all of you. Remember that only those who have ears and eyes that will hear and see will understand. The rest will only hear a great number of speaking words crossing your path. There will not be the level of understanding to know what it is that I am sharing with you on this day."

When Grandfather paused once again, we could see that all eyes went from those who were sitting close to them to those who were not sitting close to them. All present were trying to see which ones who were among them would be able to understand these speaking words. No one wanted to be among the group that did not understand. All present who had heard the beginning of these things that Grandfather had brought to them realized the importance of what they would mean to all of our people.

"As it was in the times of the Great Council of Seven when Hyan was chosen as the one who would speak for those who were walking a life path with the Earth Mother, and it was in the times when Two Elks and Morning Wind were walking a life path with the Earth Mother…so it is now.

"There are many things that are available in this life path that we are walking with the Earth Mother that make one's path very easy to walk through.

These things have taken away much of the hard work required to have a place dry in the storms, warm during the sleeping season, and eating places filled with food to eat.

"The way of the life path that we are all walking now with the Earth Mother is no longer the way that it once was. There are things that make our lives so much easier now than they once were. Because of these things, there is much more time available to all who travel their path to do the things that they enjoy doing.

"It is because of this easing of our toils in the life paths that another cycle of the balance of the life path with the Earth Mother has come to all of us. From this new cycle that we are in, there will be no escaping from it by any of us who will be with the Earth Mother. This new cycle of the balance of the life path is what has been given to me so that I may share it with all of you who are gathered on this land. These speaking words that I will share with all of you must be shared with the others of your villages as well. The time has come to remember what it is that we as a people must do once again so that our way and our life paths may continue to exist within this domain of the Earth Mother."

Once again, Cheeway and I looked over the entire gathering and we could see that there was not one sound that was coming from anyone. Even the wind spirit was not making himself known and all things both great and small realized the importance of this message that Grandfather was bringing to them.

Grandfather was standing in the middle of the ceremonial circle looking at all of the faces that were there. He was making sure that he had all of their attention because what he had to share was that important.

"Because these times have become much easier for all who will walk a life path with the Earth Mother, we will see many more spirits who will come to the Earth Mother. Many of them will be walking a life path with her for the first time.

"It has always been in times such as these that those spirits who are either too timid, or too lazy, will come to gather up those things that they feel they can learn in an easier way. They will only come to learn those things that will minimally advance their own spirits, but they will try to take as much as they can without doing the work that is needed for it.

"We all know that to gain anything without performing the required work for it does not bring us anything but a temporary gain. Without the required work being performed by the body, the spirit does not get the chance to come through and assist in those things that need to be done. It is only when the body becomes so tired, almost to the point of exhaustion that the spirit will come to its assistance. It is only in this way that the door that exists between the body and the spirit is opened. Under these circumstances, it will be opened without any need for the warrior that lives within each of us to do any battle.

"We have been taught that the Earth Mother has given to all of us who will come to walk a life path with her. However, for those who are coming into her domain in this generation, they will not have the ears to listen to her and because they will not have the ears to listen to her ways of attaining a higher life path, then they will resent all those who are attaining these things."

Grandfather paused for another moment and was looking around all of the faces that were being presented to him in this council gathering. I could tell that he was seeing in his mind a question that was coming to many that were seated around him.

"Many of you will ask yourselves a question. This question will be if these other new spirits who have no idea of how to listen and learn from the ways that the Earth Mother has set before them, then why can we not make them leave?

"A question similar to this one was asked by our ancestors and not very long ago. Their response to this question did not work well because we lost our freedom to travel freely in the lands of the Earth Mother. Even though we are the ones who have the choice of being able to cross on both sides of the fence around us, we are still separated from those others who are locked on the outside. In time, they will covet our lands because we have been able to keep them, as the Earth Mother would have us keep them for her children.

"In time, they will possibly win; but for now, we will live as we were meant to live.

"So, I will tell you, in answer to this question of why we do not just make them leave if they are not like us: it does not work. Just as the way that our ancestors felt about these new restrictions that were placed upon all of us in those few short generations ago, we will end up with the same results if we attempt to protect those things that we know have been given to us to keep again.

"What will we do if we cannot keep them out of our lands? What will happen to all of our people and their ways of life? Who will take care of the Earth Mother and all of her children if we are not here to do so? And if this happens," Grandfather said, as he turned slowly around to see all of the faces that were cast upon him. "If this happens, and there are no others who will care for the Earth Mother and her children?

"Well, our spoken history tells us what has happened before and I have no reason to believe that it will not be even worse if this happens again.

"The domain of the Earth Mother's will be rid of all who would come to walk a life path with her for the rest of the time that is hers. If there are no others who will come to tend her needs, it will unleash the complete fury of all of the spirits of the land.

"There will not be any who will be able to withstand this kind of fury. The spirits of the land will search out every spirit who is walking a life path with the Earth Mother and will destroy them all.

"This is what will happen if we do not make the necessary preparations for these times that are to come. I know that the spirits of the land who have delivered this message of what will happen is truth and this I will tell you now. Look around you. Look in all of the places that are high and low. Look in all of the places that are narrow and wide. Look in all of the places that you know to be deep and remember them well. They may not be with you for much longer if we do not make the necessary preparations from this day forward.

"It is a terrible thing that we would do to not only ourselves, but to all of those who had come before us if we were to hear this warning and do nothing about it.

"I tell all of you that these spirits who will come to the Earth Mother with only one thing in the front of their minds, and that is to take all that they can from her. They will not only come to those who live and are made to stay on the outside of our lands, but they will also come to us who live on both sides of the fence as well.

"We all remember the way that it was designed that we should meet our other spirit. The spirit that would come to us and we would recognize only after we had prepared ourselves in the ways of the life path with the Earth Mother.

"We were told that if this was followed, we would be assured of bringing only members from our spiritual family into this domain of the Earth Mother. In the beginning of our people's history, this was followed and all those who had come to the Earth Mother to walk a life path lived in balance and harmony with all of their surroundings.

"In the days when this was the rule, then there were no needs that were not met. There was no happiness that was not found. However, as with so many things that have been given to us to live by, we forgot how valuable this lesson was to us. We were not waiting for ourselves to be prepared in order to recognize the other spirit that was meant to join with us.

"Instead of doing this work of preparation, we had decided that it was better to get all that we could as fast as we could. This has resulted not only in our going away from this teaching that has been given to us by the Earth Mother, but it has resulted in there being many families, our own included, who have brought spirits to walk a life path with her that are not of their own spirit families.

"Because of this, we can walk into many houses where the children and the parents are stranger to each other. Because of this, we can walk into many houses where the husband and wife are strangers to each other. Because of this, there is no teaching and where there is no teaching then there can be no learning. When there is no learning, then it will only follow that there will not be any understanding either.

"When there is no understanding, then all things that will come to them will be taken for granted. All of the things that we have been taught to love and appreciate and care for will be destroyed by those who do not understand.

"This, then, is why we must make our preparations for all of those things that are upon us. If we do not do this, then we will all be just as guilty as the ones who do not possess the levels of understanding that we have. However, in our case, because we do have this level of understanding, our actions will be considered to be a much worse thing if we do not do the correct thing for the circumstances that are on us all."

Once again, Grandfather paused his speaking words to all who had come to the ceremony. As Cheeway and I looked over the faces of the ones who were in attendance, we could see that all of the faces that they had put on were in complete surprise to what had been shared with them.

There was no kind of movement among so many who were gathered in this place. Not even their eye lids were moving and the lands that we were on had become so quiet that we could hear the sounds of those breathing.

It was customary for anyone who was speaking to be given their time uninterrupted. Those who would wish to speak to them in the form of asking questions would always wait until the one who had shared their speaking words with them had sat down. This was the sign that they were finished with the speaking words.

If they left the place where they had been sharing, then it would mean that they would not answer any questions from anyone. However, if they would sit down on this place, then all that had gathered before them would know that they would be willing to answer any questions that would come to them.

As Cheeway and I looked over the faces of those who were gathered in this place, we could see that their eyes were telling us that they were wishing that Grandfather was finished with these speaking words that he had brought to them. Already, we could see that all of those who were here were feeling the weight of the truth that was in his speaking words. They did not know if they would be able to contain any more on this day, and in this place.

We could see that Grandfather, too, had seen this in all of the faces of our people. However, he did not move from this place. He knew the importance of what it was that he was shown and he was not finished yet.

Grandfather, seeing that all of the speaking words that he had brought with him to share with all who were present, saw that they were all still able to follow the direction that he was taking them.

"There is hope for these things that we are to do," he continued.

"Even though we will need to build a fence, it will not be one that will be able to be seen by any eyes others have. This fence will be one that will be built by the collective minds of all those among our people who have advanced their spirits sufficiently.

"This fence will be made for the protection of all the things that our people hold as sacred. We must keep these things more sacred than we have ever done before. We must pull down the veil of secrecy to many of the things that we have before left in the open because of the danger of having so many who would only misuse our knowledge walk among us.

"Two Elks and Morning Wind have shared with me that the generation that is very young on this day we are together, will have great help for them as they continue to walk with the Earth Mother.

"They have told me that there will be many of our spirit family members in this generation. They will find their other spirit that will join with them. In doing so, they will become as one and will hold our truth to themselves until the time comes for them to be known by others.

"This then is our hope of continuing as a people. This then is our hope for the future of all that we hold as truth within the domain of the Earth Mother. It is because of this that there is a chance for all things that we know to be true to not be taken away from us."

Pausing once again, Grandfather looked over the faces of those who had gathered around him. He could see that the heavy weight of the speaking words that they had heard him share with them was lightened by what he had just shared with them. He knew that by the looks that were on their faces, that he had followed the instructions that Two Elks and Morning Wind had given him very well.

Grandfather was very pleased when he saw this. He knew that all of those who had gathered in this place were now ready to accept those truths that he was going to give to them.

"We call it 'When Spirits Touch'. It is a time when all of those events that needed to be learned by a spirit have been worked through and learned from. It is a time when all of the learning turns into understanding and the spirit knows that they are ready to cross the great spirit waters to return to the waiting place once again.

"The spirit knows that if they were to travel across the great spirit waters to the waiting place, that they would take many great blessings from the Earth Mother with them.

"However, before these spirits are allowed to cross these great spirit waters, they are confronted by those of their own spirit family and are given a choice.

"This choice will come to them from the spirit of their spirit family that is the closest to them at the time. They will inform this spirit that they have accomplished all that they intended to and that they may rejoin the rest of their spirit family across the great spirit waters if they wish.

"However, because they will have additional time that they may still spend among the Earth Mother, they will be offered the additional choice of staying in the life path they are walking until the remainder of the time left to them with the Earth Mother is over.

"They will be told that the choice is theirs to make but if they will stay with the Earth Mother for the rest of the time that they have been given, they will recognize the one spirit that will be good for them because they have prepared themselves. They will be told that if they decide to remain with the Earth Mother, that they will be able to join with this other spirit.

"When this joining of these two spirits takes place, our people have called this 'When Spirits Touch', then all that we have held will be shared with many by them."

As Grandfather finished these speaking words, he could see that they understood this term 'When Spirits Touch.' However, he could see that there were many among this group that had gathered in this place who were not so familiar with this term and he decided that it would be a good thing to expand on this point for them.

"When two spirits touch, there is great excitement in all of the domain of the Earth Mother. It is a cause for there to be celebration because two spirits have joined as one. The ways of our people tell us that all who will be around them will feel the love and peace that they bring with them.

"These two spirits have performed all that was required for them to advance. To see them and to be around them is to feel many blessings that have been given to them by the Earth Mother herself.

"When two spirits touch, it will be a sign that they have successfully advanced their spirits to a place where they are able to understand more of the life path that not only they walk but also those of others. Because they will have this higher level of understanding, they will be able to assist our people in maintaining all of those things that we hold as sacred teachings by the Earth Mother.

"We will know them by the things that will come to them. They will be the ones who we as a people will be guided toward as we continue to search for the many answers that we look for to advance our own spirits. We will know these spirits who have touched by the good feelings of love and peace that they will bring to all they come into contact with. We will know these spirits who have touched by the kind of quests that they will consider to be important in the life path they are walking.

"Their quests that they will be attempting to achieve will be of the highest order. The benefits that will accrue from their successful completion of them will benefit all that will walk a life path with the Earth Mother.

"This is how we will know them. Know this, the reason that they are so important to all of the things that we hold as true is because they have the understanding not to misuse those things that we consider sacred. All of the things that we will share with them will be accepted with the level of under-standing that is required by our wise ones in this generation that I am from.

"However, the generation that is going to bring about these spirits who will touch is not ready yet, but these new and lazy spirits have begun to arrive within the domain of the Earth Mother already. Some of them are even among our own people now. Both sides, those whose spirits will touch and the others, are very young now, but in a few short growing seasons, both spirit groups will be ready to make their mark within this dominion.

"As it is with all things that are within the domain of the Earth Mother, the takers will advance much more quickly than the givers. However, the takers will not ever be satisfied with what they will get because the path that they are on is one that is not ever satisfied with what it has. Those who are on the takers path do not appreciate anything of what they have and because of this, nothing ever stays with them for a long time. Those things they will have will be from the expense of the work of others. They will always be looking for something else that they may take while they are walking a life path with the Earth Mother. You will know them in this way.

"Those numbers of the ones who have come to the Earth Mother and have been destined to be among those whose spirits will touch will be much smaller in their numbers. When they are young, they will appear to be much weaker in the strength of their spirits than the takers. However, do not be fooled by their appearance of weakness because it is not weak at all. They will only give the appearance of this because they are continuing to learn within themselves. In time, there will emerge a spirit whose strength will not be equaled by any you have ever seen in the life path that you are walking.

"The strength that they will possess will come from the knowing of many things. Those things that they will know of have come from their many seasons of working through lessons that have been given to them. Their strength comes to them from the understanding that they have gained by working through all of these events that have come their way. They will gain strength with each obstacle that they will overcome. The spiritual strength that they will possess will cause a great fear to the takers when they are confronted by them.

"However, because the takers who are already among us do not require the great amount of seasons in order for them to be ready to perform, they will be performing their quests at a far earlier time than the ones whose spirits will touch.

"It is because they will not be ready to perform the task of being the keepers of those things that we consider sacred that we will be required to place a fence around our information, wisdom, and knowledge so that it may not be revealed before it is time.

"This fence will be able to be taken down when this group of family spirits is prepared. This time will become obvious to all of us who are gathered on this land. We will see them as they will walk and speak among all of us. We will be able to see their strength and unity and when we will see this, it will make us feel good.

"Those whose spirits touch will become their helpers of our people. You will know them by the way they will see things. The things that they see will have the same values as those things that we will see. They will know our ways and we will be able to understand theirs. We will feel no fear or hostility from them and they will bring us great peace, love, and clarity from their under-standing ways of the life path that they will be walking.

"So, now is the time to prepare. This time is upon us. However, soon will come the time when these spirits will touch. They will be able to give us more understanding from our own song legends and spirit paintings and writings than we have now.

"We have all arrived at this point in our histories and we should be grateful to the Great Spirit for allowing us all to share this time with each other.

"My sharing with you from these speaking words that I have been given is done."

Finishing his speaking words, Grandfather stayed in the same place on this land he had been in while sharing this knowledge with all who had gathered before him. He paused for a brief moment to look at all of the faces that were looking at him, then with a slight movement of his right hand that went across the level of the lands that we were all on, he sat down and remained silent.

Those who were also seated in their places knew this sign. It was the sign that he was now willing to answer any questions from what he had shared with them.

However, there were no noises or sounds of speaking words coming from any of those who had gathered on this land for this occasion. There was only the silence of waiting that had fallen over this land that we were on. The only sound that was to be heard during this time was the sound of the wind spirit carrying its messages from the Earth Mother to her children as it would pass through the tall trees that were always standing in their places on this land.

Grandfather saw that there would be no question from any who were gathered and slowly rose from his sitting position that he had taken and walked out of the circle.

As he sat down on this place that was marked for him, the silence of this large group was broken by the sound of the voice of the spirit caller. He had remained seated in his place next to the inner circle and he began to sing:

> "Oh Great Spirit
> You who know us all by our names and our deeds
> Keep us with you in these times of our need
> Let us stand in your shadow of life so that all with in time be one
> Loving Earth Mother, let us stay
> In this place of yours where your children play
> Teach us your giving ways
> Let us teach them to our young

Bless all of the seasons that we will spend with you
So we may return to you in the ways that are ours
Thank you for your children
May we learn to love you as they do
Let us keep safe your truths
Help us to guard them
In the ways that we will guard our young."

The spirit caller's singing voice had stopped and still there was not one voice among all that had gathered in this land. When the last echo of his singing words had crossed over the last breath of the wind spirit, all of those who had come to this land for this occasion silently rose from their seated position and began to leave.

Cheeway and I could see that Grandfather, Two Bears, and their friend remained seated, so Cheeway and I did the same. This event that we were able to see was a great one. By the same mind that has always been our peoples', they knew that the time here on this land was completed and now it was time for them all to return to their villages and begin their work.

Grandfather was looking at Cheeway and I as this was taking place. When we met his eyes with ours, we could see that he had placed a very peaceful and knowing smile on his face. We knew that this smile was for our own benefit and this made us both feel very good.

PART XII

❀

A Place Called Beginning

CHAPTER 40

❀

Spirit Hawk

On the way back to our village, Grandfather told us that sometimes these gatherings would have events such as this take place in them. He said that when these kinds of occasions would happen, they would be called a gathering of visions. It would be from the sharing of these visions that our people would always know those things that they must do.

Arriving at our village, Cheeway and I were sharing our own speaking words of these events that had taken place on the land that was high in the Jemez Mountains. We were trying to gain some understanding from what had happened. However, our efforts were broken by the sound of a voice that had come from behind us as we were sitting under the small pine tree that was located in the front of my parents' house.

"Hello, young ones," came the voice from behind our position.

Cheeway and I turned our heads to see who it was that was behind us. We were both surprised to see that it was the friend of Grandfather and Two Bears. He had been the one who had traveled to the Jemez Mountains with us.

"I am sorry that we did not have the opportunity of sharing more speaking words together in the land of our mountains. However, since I was passing this way and saw the two of you here in the yard, I thought that now might be a good time to share ourselves for awhile."

Cheeway and I were looking at him and seeing nothing of the things Grandfather had taught us to look for as being bad in another person, we gave this friend of Grandfather and Two Bears' a warm smile and invited him onto our small piece of land so that he could share the space under the pine tree with us.

Coming onto our land, he took a seat next to the both of us. Looking at each of us with eyes that we knew were going to a place that was very deep within each of us, he smiled a very peaceful smile.

"Well, it would seem as though my two good friends, Grandfather and Two Bears share yet another thing in common. I, too, can see the richness of the spirit that is lying deep within each of you.

"I am called Spirit Hawk. Grandfather and Two Bears and I have been with each other since we were much younger than each of you," came the words of Spirit Hawk.

"Spirit Hawk," I said, trying to hold a tone to my speaking words of respect. "If you have been with each other for such a long time, then how is it that neither Cheeway nor I know you? We have been with Grandfather all of our lives and to the best of our memory, we do not remember you."

Spirit Hawk looked at both of us with a knowing smile crossing the corners of his face. "Ah, but I do remember both of you. You see, I was there when Grandfather brought you both before the council that had gathered many seasons ago."

CHAPTER 41

❀

The Councils Meeting for When Spirits Touch

"What was this council?" Cheeway asked. "I do not remember it at all."

"This council that Grandfather had brought you to was at a season when neither of you had more than three seasons to the life path you are walking. It was done for more of a reason now than was understood by any of us then.

"You see, there had been a call from many of our wise ones for this council to be held. Our wise ones had been given many dreams. The dreams they had been given were showing them many spirits coming to walk a life path with the Earth Mother. In those dreams, the wise ones saw that there were many of these spirits coming to the Earth Mother with a destiny of being joined to another spirit in order to perform great quests for her.

"Of those wise ones, three of them were Grandfather, Two Bears, and myself. We each brought one child to this council so that those who would be in attendance could gaze into their spirit and see if what these dreams that we had been shown were true or if they were just another way of wishing for something good to happen during the life path we were all walking with the Earth Mother.

"There were many in attendance on this day and each of the members of the council of the wise had brought one child with them. It was truly a great joy that crossed all of our hearts on that day when we knew that these dreams had come to us in their true form and not in a form that was created from our hopes.

"However, because we could see that within each of these small little spirit walkers we had brought with us that a potential of joining with another spirit in the life path that they were walking was not in the normal set of what our people had seen before, we knew that there was a designed reason for this.

"We knew that the Great Spirit would not allow so many with such strength walk a life path with the Earth Mother together unless there was a great need for it.

"This, then, became the quest of the members of this council of the wise. It has become one of our most important quests that we have ever taken up. During the council meeting, it was decided that all that were gathered take the one that they had brought with them and teach them in the ways of our ancestors and this is what we have been doing ever since that time in those seasons long ago.

"This result of the council that I have shared with you has been shared to those in the mountains that had gathered for the great ceremony. All of the reasons, visions, guidance, and help that we have received were shared with all that were gathered on that day. This answer that we had been given as to why there were so many spirits who were coming was shared with all who were present that day by the speaking words Grandfather shared with them.

"However, we did not want to share these truths until we could make all of these children who had come to us ready to accept those things that they would be capable of understanding. Then we knew that their strength would begin to grow sufficiently enough so that they would be able to stand on their own.

"This is what Grandfather has been doing with the two of you. The others of our wise have been doing the same with the spirits who have come to them.

"So, I remember the both of you and even though neither of you remember me, I thought that I would come by this land you were taking time on and see how both of you were developing."

Spirit Hawk remained silent but very attentive to all things that were going on around him. We could see a quality that was in his eyes that told us that he was a spirit who was very intelligent and could see things that he would consider to be of importance very quickly.

"Spirit Hawk," I said. "Why was it so important to know that these dreams that were being given to the old were true? Could these wise ones just not believe the dream spirits that had brought them to them?"

"This is what should have been," Spirit Hawk returned. "However, with so many messages that were coming to all of our wise ones during this time, we were not sure if this one was true or not. With so many great dreams and visions that were being given to all of us, we wanted to make a test to see if the one that told us that many spirits would come to us in the generation that both of you are in would become 'When Spirits Touch'.

"Once we found this to be true, we knew then that the rest of these visions and dreams would be true as well. This is why we chose to perform the deeds that we did on this council meeting that I have shared with you.

"This is why so many seasons have been devoted to teaching all of the spirits, who have come to our people, in the ways of our ancestors and those things that we consider to be sacred. We know that it will be by the efforts of all these spirits that our way of life will not pass away.

"Knowing that our knowledge and teachings will be safe for others who will come to walk a life path brings a great peace to all of our people. All who have been and all who will be, will benefit greatly by these efforts that are yet to be made."

"Spirit Hawk," I asked, "are those who have been destined to be joined as When Spirits Touch only among our own people?"

"No!" Spirit Hawk answered very quickly. "However, we did not have any means available to us that would allow us to reach all who had come to the Earth Mother. Those others we knew would be living their life path on the outside of the places that we call our own lands.

"We can only hope that the ones we will teach will be able to reach these other spirits who have come to the Earth Mother for the same reason in some way.

"Whatever way this will be, it will take its place when its time has come. Once its time has come, there will be no stopping the knowledge and wisdom that has been given to the others to share. This we continue to hope for, so this will be what will happen."

Spirit Hawk closed his eyes for a brief moment and we knew that he was putting his speaking words together so that he would be able to share them with us both correctly.

"Your generation is only the beginning of the entry of When Spirits Touch. There is a new way of understanding that will soon be crossing the entire domain of the Earth Mother's and the generation that both of you are in is only the beginning of this.

"When the time comes for this first of When Spirits Touch, there will be a great call that will be heard throughout the entire domain of the Earth Mother. This call will begin with only one small child of the Earth Mother but it will be heard by many others of her children and they will continue to tell their stories that the first of When Spirits Touch has begun.

"The ones who already have come among us are only the beginning, as I have shared with you. Others will follow and the visions that I have seen tell me that there will be such a great number of them, that their strength and deeds will change the entire domain of what we now know as the one of the Earth Mother.

"The additional learning and understanding that will occur from those spirits who join will be of such great measure, that all who walk in this domain will only marvel in the beginning and think that they are dreaming that this is actually happening.

"You see," Spirit Hawk continued, "it is When Spirits Touch is reached, that there is such a rebirth of love and understanding and peace that it will cause a great outflow to pour from them. This will continue for as long as they will walk a life path with the Earth Mother.

"This outflow cannot be ignored by any who will come into contact with them nor can it be explained away by any of the speaking words that are known either. It is something that must only be accepted and nothing more.

"When the first of the When Spirits Touch is attained, then other spirits will be blessed from the light of understanding that they will share with each other. There will be something that will be awakened within each of them when this happens. They will know when they have been prepared and will go forth to seek out their other spirit that has been destined to be joined to them.

"This complete process will continue until there is a sacred ring that will go completely around the Earth. When this sacred ring will be completed, then the things that are held as truth will then be understood and in a way that will advance all of their spirits.

"All of those things that they will know to be important to them and their spiritual advancement will be understood. Those things that are not necessary to them and their spiritual advancement will be discarded and they will not devote any more of their time on them.

"From the one joining of When spirits Touch will come many. From those many will come the sacred ring that will encircle the Earth, and from the completing of this sacred ring, will come the love and the peace that all who walk a life path with the Earth Mother have heard of. This is the reason that our people have given such a great amount of importance to this."

CHAPTER 42

❀

We Stayed Behind To Help

"Spirit Hawk," Cheeway asked, "both Grandfather and Two Bears have told us that they have been in the When Spirits Touch only to later be left behind to continue with the quests that have been given to them for the Earth Mother. Have you reached this place as well?"

"Yes, I have, and I, too, have been left behind. However, I know the reason that I have decided to remain with the Earth Mother. It is the same as Grandfather and Two Bears had. We stayed behind to teach those who were given into our keeping."

"Who is that?" Cheeway asked.

"That is not important now. What is important is that you both continue to walk that path that has been set before you so that when the time comes for your recognition, then you will both be ready."

"Spirit Hawk," I asked, "how is it that, if all three of you have been to the When Spirits Touch, the sacred circle had not been formed around the Earth Mother before now?"

Spirit Hawk looked at me and I could tell by the depth of his eyes that he was looking straight into my spirit.

"It was not time," came his answer to me, as he cleared the look of his penetrating eyes with a warm smile.

"There will be additional blessings that will come from these spirits once they join and become When Spirits Touch," came a voice from behind us.

When Cheeway and I turned around to see who was the owner of this voice, we were surprised to see that it was Grandfather and Two Bears. They had also walked to the fence that was behind us and were waiting to be invited onto our land where my parents' house sat.

I quickly made the welcoming sign to them and they crossed over the same path that Spirit Hawk had crossed when he first entered this place where we had been sitting. As they approached our place where we were sitting, they also took up sitting positions that were on either side of the one that Spirit Hawk was at.

"These additional blessings that will come to us will be because these two spirits who have become one will share much knowledge and understanding with us. This will mean that it will not be from the eyes of a male or a female, but it will come from the eyes of both as they will continue to share with all who will come to them. This will give us a greater understanding to all things that have been and will give a clearer meaning to the path that we are walking," Grandfather said, as he was looking at both Cheeway and myself with a very tender smile that had come over his face.

"When two spirits touch," Grandfather said, as he bent his head to the direction of where the spirit wind was coming from as it crossed our lands, "all who are within the domain of the Earth Mother's will know that this has happened. Look at her children who will come to you and their presence will tell you when you are with the one who is the spirit that you have been destined to be joined with.

"Listen to this child of the Earth Mother's because it will be this life that will announce to all present that these two spirits have touched and there love is destined to grow in this land they will walk. They will be the one who will announce that where there was once two that there is now one and for them When Spirits Touch has begun."

"When you have touched this other spirit," Two Bears continued, with the same style of speaking words as Grandfather had been sharing, "you will see many things that you had seen before but they will all appear to you as new. You will both look at the same things that you have both seen before and you will both see the newness that will come from them to each of you. The reason for this is because you have each accepted your strengths that each of you has brought to each other. It has opened this awareness more than you could ever perceive as being possible before both of you had touched."

"When you reach When Spirits Touch," Spirit Hawk continued, with the same way of sharing that Grandfather and Two Bears had done, "and they begin their quest to become one within the other, along their way there will be many things of the past that had once held each of them back. These things will begin to fall away from themselves. These things will fall away from them because they are no longer important to hold onto. As each one of these things is released, there will be more room for the other one who they have touched to come into them with all of the spiritual strengths and understanding that they have brought to them. This additional space will also allow their love to grow as they continue to the path that will lead them to become one with each other in this life path that they are walking."

CHAPTER 43

❀

Waiting For When Spirits Touch

When these speaking words had been finished, all three of them, Grandfather, Two Bears, and Spirit Hawk, rose from their sitting positions and turned away from Cheeway and I. They began to walk into the direction where the sun was going down over our lands on the mesa. Cheeway and I continued to sit in our positions and watch them as they walked away.

We did not know where they were going to, but we did know where they had been and what they had shared with both of us. We knew that the seasons that were ahead of both of us, and the path that we would travel among the Earth Mother and her children, would be filled with events that, if worked through, would lead us both to the other spirit who had also come to the Earth Mother to join with each of us.

As we continued to sit on our place that was under the small pine tree, Cheeway and I were thinking of how easy it would be to pass the one we had been destined to meet and be joined with if we were not prepared for this.

The rest of that day, and for many others that were to come, we would always look to all of the events that would come to us as something that we would learn from. We would learn from them as we would learn to work through them, and the place where we would continue to get our strength of working through them would come from the knowing that all of this was in preparation so that we would be able to meet the one we had been prepared for in this life path that we were walking with the Earth Mother, the spirits of the land, and all of the children of the Earth Mother.

As this day over the lands of our people on the mesa was slowly passing itself by us, Cheeway and I could feel that we, too, were passing out of one level of understanding and into another. We could feel this change as it was taking root deep within each of us. We knew this change was good. We knew that this path we were walking was the right one. We knew that all of our efforts would help us. That by doing this for ourselves, we would be helping our own people…in a way that would ensure that our way of life would not pass from this domain of the Earth Mother where many spirits would come to share a life path with her.

About the Author

❀

Patrick "Speaking Wind" Quirk, a Native American author, lecturer, and publisher, was raised by Grandfather, Two Bears, and White Eagle of the Pueblo People. He knew them as Spirit Callers, but in today's terms we would call them "SHAMAN". He, and his brothers, Cheeway and Nahe, were raised in the mountains of northern New Mexico by Grandfather and Two Bears for almost twenty years of their early life. This is where they were introduced to the ways of the spirit.

However, these teachings were to be put asleep for a time, and were not to be remembered until the time was right. But before the time was right, Grandfather, Two Bears, and White Eagle left, with their bodies, and several years later, Cheeway, and Nahe, ended their journey with the Earth Mother as well. That left Speaking Wind alone, to sort and process, what he had been given to share.

When Speaking Wind, Cheeway, and Nahe were very young, they were placed in a boarding school for several years. And this became the first of their experiences from having the control of others attempt to bury their spiritual beliefs. During their boarding school experience, they were not allowed to speak their peoples language, or practice their spirituality. And there were placed on them many scars of abuse for breaking these rules.

During the boarding school years, they, as well as others who were either mixed, or full blooded Native Americans, were not taught to read or write. Instead, they were marched to the back of the school and picked up by residents, then taken to their private homes, and farms, where they would work, for no pay. They would be returned to the boarding school, only, when it was time for them to learn of its religion.

However, they had asked too many questions from the teachings of Grandfather, Two Bears and White Eagle. Questions the teachers could not answer. So, they were labeled as "Spawns Of Satan" and forced to leave so they would not influence the children who were not following the "devil's evil ways".

When Speaking Wind, Nahe, and Cheeway entered the public school system, they could not read or write. They had not been taught. So not only the teachers, but the students, called them dumb Indians.

That left a mark on them, and gave them the determination to pursue their academic goals. Cheeway completed his doctorate and worked as one of the lead archeologists in the Yucatan Peninsula uncovering many of the ancient writings and civilizations that related to the sacred writings of the Pueblo People.

Nahe pursued a career in law enforcement, then went on to become Sheriff in a small town in New Mexico.

Speaking Wind attained two undergraduate degrees, two graduate degrees, and completed one half of his doctorate. He taught in the school of business, at the University Of Phoenix, then worked as a consultant in Asia, and for almost sixteen years, as a consultant in Europe.

However, for Speaking Wind, all of this was to end in 1993 when he died and was taken to the lands of The Ancient Ones. This is where he was not only reunited with Grandfather, Two Bears, White Eagle, Cheeway and Nahe, but also the "GREAT MESSENGER". This was when the "GREAT MESSENGER" gave Speaking Wind a message to bring back...a message that was to be shared with all who had the eyes to see, the ears to hear, the heart to feel, and the willingness of spirit to understand. It is a message of love, a message of hope, but most of all, it is a message that can replace fear, with understanding, for everyone.

It was at this time, when Speaking Wind was told it was time to begin his work, and return to Turtle Island (The Continental United States) with his son, White Raven. Speaking Wind, and his son, have traveled together since White Raven was six.

For the next five years, Speaking Wind and White Raven toured the United States holding seminars and lectures. In these, Speaking Wind presented Native American spiritual practices and performed healing ceremonies to all those who were ready to receive them. One of the most compelling of the ceremonies Patrick performed were the spirit drummings. During some of these, a dimensional "portal" would open and people looking into the eye of a stranger would be able to see an aspect of their own spirit as they truly were. Many times this image would be something that needed to be worked on.

But it was the drumming at Kinlock, one of the sacred areas in the land now known as Bankhead National Forest, which always resulted in different manifestations. Many times, people heard native flute music playing. And on more than one occasion, several people admitted to actually seeing images of the Old Ones.

Times were very fast paced for Patrick during the 1990's. Years of a grueling seminar schedule and many overnight hours of working on his latest manuscripts finally took their toll. On December 22nd, 1998, Speaking Wind crossed over. Or, as Patrick would say, he allowed his robes to fall away and leave the Earth Mother.

Since his departure, his physical presence has been greatly missed. But his spirit has visited many of us. And while his teachings are carried forward in the form of his books, manuscripts, and tapes, it is his personal impact on a small circle of friends and seminar acquaintances that will remain with us for the rest of our lives.

Washte Speaking Wind.

www.ingramcontent.com/pod-product-compliance
Lightning Source LLC
Chambersburg PA
CBHW031150270326
41931CB00006B/217